Coping with Disability

ISSUES

Volume 135

Series Editor

Lisa Firth

 *Independence*

Educational Publishers
Cambridge

First published by Independence
PO Box 295
Cambridge CB1 3XP
England

© Independence 2007

British Library Cataloguing in Publication Data
Coping with Disability – (Issues Series)
I. Firth, Lisa II. Series
362.4'0941

ISBN 978 1 86168 387 8

Printed in Great Britain
MWL Print Group Ltd

Cover
The illustration on the front cover is by
Don Hatcher.

CONTENTS

Chapter One: Disability Issues

Disability issues	1
Disability in the UK	2
Adjusting to disability	4
Benefits	5
Disability facts	6
Transport options for disabled people	7
Young carers	10
'Hidden Lives'	11
Ross's story	12
The Disability Discrimination Act (DDA)	22
The campaign for real choice	23
'Lack of choice' for disabled children	24
International disability facts	25
Disabled treaty to reverse years of neglect	26
'Institutional disablism' is rife in Britain	28
Recognising disablism	29
Living with a label	30
Disabled people on TV	32

Chapter Two: Equality and Rights

Equality rights	13
The disability symbol	14
Diversity good for business	14
Workplace prejudice	15
Disabled people continue to bear brunt of UK poverty	16
Disability and employment statistics	16
The cost of poverty	17
Social care	18
The care gap	20
Resources for disabled children	21

Chapter Three: Learning Disabilities

Information on learning disabilities	33
Managing a learning disability	34
Not seen, not heard	35
Special Educational Needs	36
Learning together for the better	37
Key Facts	40
Glossary	41
Index	42
Additional Resources	43
Acknowledgements	44

Introduction

Coping with Disability is the one hundred and thirty-fifth volume in the **Issues** series. The aim of this series is to offer up-to-date information about important issues in our world.

Coping with Disability looks at disability issues, equality and rights, and learning disabilities.

The information comes from a wide variety of sources and includes:
Government reports and statistics
Newspaper reports and features
Magazine articles and surveys
Website material
Literature from lobby groups
and charitable organisations.

It is hoped that, as you read about the many aspects of the issues explored in this book, you will critically evaluate the information presented. It is important that you decide whether you are being presented with facts or opinions. Does the writer give a biased or an unbiased report? If an opinion is being expressed, do you agree with the writer?

Coping with Disability offers a useful starting-point for those who need convenient access to information about the many issues involved. However, it is only a starting-point. Following each article is a URL to the relevant organisation's website, which you may wish to visit for further information.

* * * * *

Disability issues

Information from Scope

Numbers of disabled people

We cannot be certain about the number of disabled people in Great Britain, as there is a range of different statistics. The main reasons for the variations are due to when and how the information was collected. For example, did people complete a questionnaire themselves, or did someone else decide whether they 'counted' as disabled?

According to the 2001 census results there are 10.8 million people (of all ages) in the UK who have a long-term health problem or disability, which limits their daily activities or the work they could do. They make up 18.5% of the population.

Government research estimates that there are 8.6 million disabled adults (aged 16+) living in private households in the UK, (i.e. 20% of the adult population) and nearly 400,000 disabled children under the age of 16. This accounts for approximately one in 38 of all children in the population.

The total number is likely to rise further with an increasingly elderly population, as the likelihood of disability increases with age.

Discrimination and attitudes

Disabled people continue to face discrimination and difficulties imposed by society in every area of their lives. The common experiences of disabled people are of rejection and enormous difficulty in taking part in even the most ordinary activities such as shopping, going to the cinema or to the pub.

Discrimination is present in education and employment, often leading to lifelong dependence on welfare benefits.

Many polling stations are inaccessible; therefore disabled people are denied the right to vote on equal terms with non-disabled people. In addition, disabled people are forced into dependence, suffer humiliation and struggle with an inaccessible environment every day.

As a consequence, many disabled people give up the struggle of attempting to take part in society and stay at home.

The exclusion of disabled people from society means that some non-disabled people have never met a disabled person and therefore do not have the opportunity to develop opinions and attitudes about them based on personal experience.

Lack of awareness and fear of the unknown are compounded by the predominantly negative media images of disabled people and of disability generally. For example, in a survey conducted by The Leonard Cheshire Foundation, nearly one-third of people questioned thought that wheelchair-users were 'less intelligent'; and 44% of

opinion leaders thought that using a wheelchair would present a major obstacle to gaining employment. Such misconceptions lead to a vicious circle of rejection, discrimination and exclusion.

Language

What we say both reflects and shapes the way we think. The language we use about disability is an important way of influencing our own and society's attitudes.

Words and phrases to avoid include: handicapped person, spastic, wheelchair-bound, sufferer, the disabled.

Use the following instead: disabled person, has cerebral palsy, wheelchair-user, has an impairment.

Social versus medical model of disability

Behaviour towards disabled people is governed by the picture or 'model' of disability that others carry in their minds. These models, in turn, affect the way in which society is organised.

The two main models are:

⇨ The medical model sees disability as an illness and disabled people as patients in need of a cure so that they can fit into 'normal' society. The emphasis is on the condition rather than the person.

⇨ The social model recognises disabled people as equals who are battling against very unequal odds i.e. society's attitudes. The emphasis is on society's responsibilities and changing attitudes rather than the disabled person's problem.

⇨ The above information is reprinted with kind permission from Scope. Visit www.scope.org.uk for more information.

© Scope

Disability in the UK

Information from the Economic and Social Research Council

This information provides an overview of the issues relating to disability in the UK. It is designed to introduce the topic rather than be a comprehensive survey.

The UK Disability Discrimination Act (1995) defines a disabled person as someone with 'a physical or mental impairment which has a substantial and long-term adverse effect on his (sic) ability to carry out normal day-to-day activities'. Disabilities are diverse and range in severity. They may be either visible or invisible, or both.

> **Disabilities are diverse and range in severity. They may be either visible or invisible, or both**

The key types of disability relate to problems with mobility, sensory mechanisms, learning and communication difficulties, mental health issues and hidden disabilities like diabetes, epilepsy and heart disease. Many of these forms of disability are treatable or may be alleviated by broader changes in social perceptions.

Disability in the UK

It is estimated that there are about 9.8 million people in the UK with some form of disability – one in seven of the population. At the last count, in 1996, there were 750,000 wheelchair users in the UK. In 2002-03, 19 per cent of men and 13 per cent of women reported having hearing difficulties, and in 2004 55,000 people were registered as deaf. In 2003, 157,000 people were registered as blind. In terms of hidden disabilities, there are about 1.8 million diabetics in the UK and over 350,000 people with epilepsy, for example.

Demographics

The incidence and experience of disability differs by socio-economic status, gender, age, religion and ethnicity. As would be expected, the odds of being disabled increase significantly with advancing age. In England the likelihood of having a disability is eight times higher among those aged 75 and over than among those aged 16-44. Only 28 per cent of wheelchair users are under 60.

People in lower social-economic classes are more likely both to be, and to become disabled, and disabled people are more likely either to be or become lower class. Figures from 2001 show that eight per cent of people in Social Class I were disabled, compared to 24 per cent of people in Social Class V.

In 2000, rates of severe disability among children were consistently higher for boys than for girls (11 per 10,000 of the male population under 17, compared with five per 10,000 of females of the same age group). However, rates of female disability are higher for older age groups. This is because of a longer survival rate of women with disabilities rather than a difference in incidence.

Amongst different religious groups in the UK in 2001, age-standardised rates of disability were highest for Muslims. Almost a quarter of Muslim females (24%) had a disability, as did one in five (21%) of Muslim males. Jewish people had the lowest rates of disability (13% for both males and females).

Regional patterns

The geography of disability in the UK shows marked regional variations. As the graph 'Disability by region' shows, while only 17 per cent of households in the South East accommodate one or more disabled adult under the pension age, in the North East this rises to 27 per cent. This is consistent with regional patterns of other health indices.

Disability discrimination and labour market participation

38 per cent of men and 37 per cent of women with a disability were in paid employment, compared to 81 per cent of men and 69 per cent of women with no disability. Unemployment rates for disabled people are about twice as high as those of people

---

38 per cent of men and 37 per cent of women with a disability were in paid employment, compared to 81 per cent of men and 69 per cent of women with no disability

---

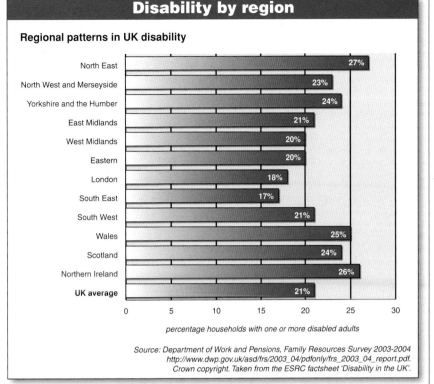

Disability by region

Regional patterns in UK disability

Region	Percentage
North East	27%
North West and Merseyside	23%
Yorkshire and the Humber	24%
East Midlands	21%
West Midlands	20%
Eastern	20%
London	18%
South East	17%
South West	21%
Wales	25%
Scotland	24%
Northern Ireland	26%
UK average	21%

percentage households with one or more disabled adults

Source: Department of Work and Pensions, Family Resources Survey 2003-2004
http://www.dwp.gov.uk/asd/frs/2003_04/pdfonly/frs_2003_04_report.pdf.
Crown copyright. Taken from the ESRC factsheet 'Disability in the UK'.

---

without a disability. In part this disparity results from the large number of disabled people who are permanently unable to work. 46 per cent of men and 34 per cent of women of working age with a disability were unable to work, compared with two per cent of men and one per cent women with no disability.

In 2003 2.5 million people in the UK received financial support through the disability living allowance. In 2002 the UK spent 2.5 per cent of its total GDP on disability benefits. As the graph 'European spending on disability benefits' shows, this is slightly above the European average of 2.2 per cent but less than Sweden, which spends 4.3 per cent.

Although attitudes are changing as a result of the Disability Discrimination Act (1995), there is evidence that the low level of labour market participation amongst disabled people is also due to tacit discrimination on the part of employers, and on practical difficulties in getting to work.

For example, in a survey carried out by the Disability Rights Commission (DRC), 46 per cent of the public thought that disabled people were still treated unfairly by society. Furthermore, some 32 per cent of all economically inactive working-age disabled people said they would like to be in paid employment compared to 26 per cent of non-disabled people.

In a further survey, the DRC discovered that 73 per cent of disabled people with mobility and sensory impairments in the UK have difficulty accessing goods and services. Primarily this is due to steps, heavy doors and a lack of parking and lifts. In the British Social Attitudes Survey (2000) over 65 per cent of people thought that more could be done to make shops and services more accessible to disabled people.

⇨ The above information is reprinted with kind permission from the Economic and Social Research Council. Visit www.esrc.ac.uk for more information.

© ESRC

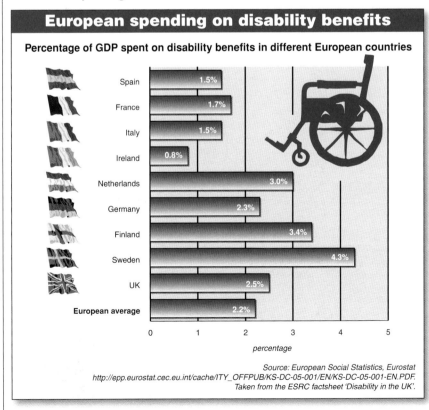

European spending on disability benefits

Percentage of GDP spent on disability benefits in different European countries

Country	Percentage
Spain	1.5%
France	1.7%
Italy	1.5%
Ireland	0.8%
Netherlands	3.0%
Germany	2.3%
Finland	3.4%
Sweden	4.3%
UK	2.5%
European average	2.2%

percentage

Source: European Social Statistics, Eurostat
http://epp.eurostat.cec.eu.int/cache/ITY_OFFPUB/KS-DC-05-001/EN/KS-DC-05-001-EN.PDF.
Taken from the ESRC factsheet 'Disability in the UK'.

Adjusting to disability

Becoming disabled through illness, injury, accident or a worsening medical condition can affect many areas of people's lives. This could be family, work, money and health. This article lists some of the things you need to think about

Your doctor (GP)

Your local doctor (GP) will be central to much of the health support you receive whether you have a progressive illness (something that develops over time or in stages) or a sudden disability caused by, for example, an accident.

You may also come across doctors and consultants and their teams who specialise in certain conditions and disabilities at hospitals and clinics.

Health and social care support

Becoming disabled means you may need support from health and social care services for the first time. A health and social care assessment with the social services department of your local council is the first step.

You may be entitled to a package of support which could include home care help, disability and/or health equipment and adaptations. Direct payments allow you to arrange your own support instead of receiving it directly from your council – if you are assessed as needing help.

You may also be entitled to a grant to help you adapt your home or be offered alternative accommodation such as supported housing.

Your local council will have its own website detailing the support available to you at a local level.

Support groups and organisations

Keeping in touch with other disabled people can be a good way of getting informal advice and support – especially if you are newly disabled.

Your family and friends

Family members and friends may suddenly find themselves in a 'caring role'. They are also entitled to an assessment of their needs as a carer. They may be entitled to receive financial support such as Carer's Allowance. If you are a parent or thinking of becoming one, there is information on Directgov covering having a baby, parental support, schools and more.

Mental health

Becoming disabled can sometimes affect a person's mental health – often there is a period of adjustment needed. If you experience mental health problems your doctor or another health professional may refer you to a specialist like a psychotherapist, community psychiatric nurse or a counsellor. These professionals will work with you to help you find ways of dealing with problems you are experiencing or concerns you may have.

Financial support

If you become disabled you may be entitled to financial support to help meet extra costs as a direct result of your disability. This ranges from disability benefits, such as Disability Living Allowance, VAT relief on products and services related to your disability, Council Tax reduction through to grants to help adapt your home, where necessary.

Work, making adjustments and your rights

If you become disabled while in work there are many things you, and your employer, can do to enable you to remain in employment. You do have employment rights under the Disability Discrimination Act (DDA).

Adjustments to either the workplace, processes and your duties could include providing practical aids and technical equipment to help you, or organising a phased return to work, alternative employment within the same company or perhaps part-time work.

Whether you are in or out of work, Disability Employment Advisers at Jobcentre Plus offices or jobcentres can give you support and advice about work.

Driving and your vehicle

Whether you are a new or experienced driver, you must let the Driver and Vehicle Licensing Agency (DVLA) know about any medical condition or disability that may affect your driving.

If you become disabled you can get your vehicle adapted.

Your rights in everyday life

People who become disabled are likely to face new challenges in everyday life – from accessing services to understanding disability legislation and rights and sometimes discrimination.

⇨ The above information is reprinted with kind permission from Directgov. Please visit their website at www.direct.gov.uk for more information.

© Crown copyright

Recommended terminology

Don't use	Use
Handicapped	Disabled people
Crippled	People with impairments and long-term health conditions
The disabled	People with rights under the Disability Discrimination Act
Suffering from . . .	Has . . . arthritis, a mental health problem, diabetes etc.
Blind	Has a visual impairment. Many people who are registered blind have some sight
Deaf	Use deaf if you know someone has no hearing. If a person has some hearing use 'hearing impairment'
Mad, mental, schizoid, nutter	Has a mental health problem . . . or has depression, anxiety, a phobia, obsessive compulsive disorder, manic depression, schizophrenia etc.

Source: Disability Rights Commission

Benefits

Having a disability can lead to a lot of extra costs. They come from a number of sources:

⇨ increased day-to-day expenses: you might spend more heating your home if you are less mobile. You may need to spend extra money to look after a working dog.

⇨ large single purchases: wheelchairs, scooters, chairlifts, hoists, adaptions for your car: they are all costly buys that need to be budgeted for.

⇨ higher travel costs: you might be unable to use public transport services. If so you will need to pay for more expensive forms of transport.

⇨ reduced income: disability often has an impact on your ability to work or others' willingness to give you work. Either way, if you are unable to work or are only able to work reduced hours your monthly income will be reduced.

The social security benefits available are in many people's views inadequate compensation for the extra costs and the reduction in employment opportunities; they are, however, a right in law to all those who fit the entitlement criteria.

Disability and incapacity benefits

Attendance Allowance (AA)
For people over 65 who have needed help for at least 6 months. Applicants must need help with bodily functions (washing, dressing, eating etc.) or supervision to avoid danger to themselves or others. There are two levels of benefit depending on the level of care needed.

Disability Living Allowance (DLA)
Comprises two components, a care component and a mobility component. It is for people under the age of 65:

⇨ the care component is similar to the AA (above) but is payable to people claiming from birth until their 65th birthday. Applicants must have needed help for at least three months and be likely to require it for another six. There are three rates of payment depending on the level of care you need. If you receive the highest rate and live alone, you may be eligible to receive additional payments from the Independent Living Fund for personal care.

⇨ the mobility component is paid at two rates depending on your ability to move independently. The higher rate is for people who are virtually unable to walk and the lower is for people who can walk but who reasonably require someone with them when they are outdoors, e.g. because of a visual impairment, or epilepsy.

Industrial Injuries Disablement Benefit
Is for people injured at work. To be eligible, you must be assessed as being 'more than 14% disabled'.

Incapacity Benefit (ICB)
Is a contributory-based benefit for people who are assessed as being incapable of work. For the first six months you'll be assessed on your ability to perform your usual job. And after that you will have to take a test which assesses your capacity to do any work.

Severe Disablement Allowance (SDA)
Abolished 6th April, 2001. It is partly replaced by Incapacity Benefit for Young People.

Statutory Sick Pay (SSP)
Employed people who are sick for four or more days in a row may qualify for SSP from their employers for a maximum of 28 weeks. SSP is paid in the same way as wages.

Vaccine Damage
You might be entitled to a tax-free lump sum payment of £40,000 if you have become severely disabled as a result of specified vaccinations.

Disabled Person's Tax Credit
Although not strictly a benefit, this means-tested scheme, available to those working but on low incomes, adds a certain amount of money to your earnings whenever you're paid. If you have savings over £3,000 you'll not receive as much.

Other state benefits

Income support (IS)
Is a means-tested benefit paid as a sole benefit or to top up others. The amount you receive will depend on your income, savings and family composition. IS acts as a 'passport' to other benefits like free prescriptions.

Housing Benefit and Council Tax Benefit
Are means-tested benefits paid by local authorities using similar rules to those for Income Support to cover rent and council-tax payments.

The Social Fund
People on Income Support, income-based Jobseeker's Allowance or Disabled Person's Tax Credit are automatically entitled to maternity expenses, cold weather payments and winter fuel payments under the Regulated Social Fund.

Invalid Care Allowance (ICA)
Is a benefit that carers can claim if they care for a disabled person receiving either of the two higher DLA care rates, or either of the AA rates. To be eligible for the benefit,

they must be spending at least 35 hours a week caring.

There are also various grants, discounts and concessions available from national organisations, charities and local councils. You might be entitled, for example, to help paying for your phone or television licence. You might be eligible for a grant to help you adapt your property. You might be entitled to tax relief on some of your purchases. You might be entitled to a grant or a loan from a charity.

The benefits: how they are worked out

The amount you will receive from a certain benefit will depend upon the type of benefit it is.

Some benefits are related to a person's care or assistance needs (Attendance Allowance, the care components of the Disability Living Allowance and Invalid Care Allowance). Some are related to your level of mobility (the mobility component of the Disability Living Allowance). Some are related to your ability to work (Disability Working Allowance, Incapacity Benefit and Severe Disablement Allowance). Others are general means-tested benefits aimed at topping up your income (Income Support, Housing Benefit, Family Credit, the Social Fund).

Some benefits overlap each other, others are exclusive so that if you can get one, you cannot get another (you cannot receive AA and DLA for example) while some benefits are a 'passport' to others (if you are on Income Support, you are eligible for free prescriptions for example).

'What to do to find out more' guide

Benefits and grants are notoriously difficult to write about conclusively. State benefits change anually. Grants bestowed by local councils often depend on the area you live in and are decided upon what often appears to be an arbitrary decision made by the local disability officer.

Fortunately, if you have any queries about what you might be entitled to there are a number of good sources of help available:

⇨ you can contact local groups such as Citizens' Advice Bureau (www.

nacab.org.uk) or local disability or voluntary groups for information and advice. A larger disability-specific national organisation may be able to provide more detailed and tailored information. It might also be worth talking to your social worker, if you have one, or your local authority may have a welfare rights unit.

⇨ the Benefits Agency's (www.dwp.gov.uk) Benefit Enquiry Line can provide general information on disability and other benefits. They also offer a form-completion service for Disability Living Allowance, Attendance Allowance and Invalid Care Allowance. The Line is open 8.30am to 6.30pm Monday to Friday and 8.30am to 12.30pm on Saturday, phone: 0800 882200, textphone: 0800 243355; for Northern Ireland, tel: 0800 220674, textphone: 0800 243787, and the lines are open 9am to 5pm, Monday to Friday.

⇨ the Benefits Agency (www.dwp.gov.uk) produces a number of useful leaflets, including *Sick or Disabled: a guide to benefits for people who have a physical or mental illness or disability, including children and people who look after them*. Copies are available from Post Offices, libraries and the Benefit Agency offices.

⇨ the *Disability Rights Handbook* is an invaluable guide to all the relevant benefits and services, and includes chapters on appeals, taking benefits abroad, practical help at home, charging for residential care and compensation schemes. It is produced by the Disability Alliance and available from them at Universal House, 88-94 Wentworth Street, London E1 7SA, tel/textphone: 020 7247 8776, fax: 020 7427 8765 (ring for current prices). Disability Alliance (www.disabilityalliance.org) has a benefits advice line open Mondays and Wednesdays from 2pm-4pm. You can contact the general enquiries line for further details on 020 7247 8763.

⇨ the Child Poverty Action Group produces the comprehensive *Welfare Benefits Handbook* annually, which covers means-tested and non-means-tested benefits. They can be contacted at 94 White Lion Street, London N1 9PF, tel: 020 7837 7979, email: staff@cpag.demon.co.uk

Provided by RADAR (www.radar.org.uk)

⇨ The above information is reprinted with kind permission from youreable.com. Visit www.youreable.com for more information.

© youreable.com

Disability facts

Information from the Shaw Trust

⇨ Only 17% of disabled people were born with their disabilities (Source: Institute for Public Policy Research article 'Work for disabled people')

⇨ One in four people will be affected by mental ill health in the course of their life (Source: Mind)

⇨ Mental health problems, such as depression and anxiety, now account for more Incapacity Benefit claims than back pain (Source: Mind, *Stress and mental health in the workplace*, 2005)

⇨ One in four men and one in five women will suffer a critical illness before they are 65 (Source: Health insurance: the online guide to critical illness insurance)

⇨ Sickness absence is estimated to have cost the UK economy almost £12.2 billion in 2004 (Source: Confederation of British Industry press release, 2005).

⇨ The above information is reprinted with kind permission from the Shaw Trust. Visit www.shaw-trust.org.uk for more information.

© Shaw Trust

Transport options for disabled people

Information from Citizens' Advice

Wheelchairs

People whose walking difficulties are permanent or near permanent can get an NHS wheelchair on free loan. Details of local wheelchair services are available from GPs, local health centres and the physiotherapy or occupational therapy departments of the local hospital.

The NHS can loan more than one wheelchair if it is necessary, for example, one for using at home and the other for use at work. A wheelchair voucher scheme exists in England. Under the scheme, you may be able to get a more expensive chair of your choice by paying the difference between the value of the standard chair and that of the more expensive chair. The more expensive chair will have to be approved by the NHS. In Wales, if someone is entitled to a wheelchair but wants to 'upgrade', they must negotiate this with the local wheelchair service. In Scotland, individual health boards operate their own policies.

If you need to borrow money to buy a wheelchair you can get a loan in any of the usual ways, for example, from a bank. The Motability hire purchase scheme is available to people on certain benefits. For more information contact Motability.

Private transport

Driving

A disabled person who wants to get a provisional driving licence will have to provide information about their special needs and may have to undergo a medical examination. If a licence is refused on medical grounds you have the right to appeal to a magistrates' court (sheriff court in Scotland). In some cases, a young disabled person can get a provisional driving licence at 16 instead of 17 if they are receiving certain benefits.

Disabled people should have an assessment made of whether they will actually be able to drive and what sort of controls and equipment would be needed for a vehicle. Lessons may be available from a specially trained instructor and in a suitably adapted car. Information about assessment and instruction can be obtained from a number of organisations.

Buying or hiring a vehicle

A disabled person who wants to buy a vehicle may be able to get a discount. Contact car dealers and ask if they operate any disabled drivers' discount schemes.

Motability can sell or hire new or secondhand cars to anyone receiving the higher rate mobility component of disability living allowance or war pensioners' mobility supplement.

Some commercial hire companies offer discounts to disabled people when they hire a car or van. It is worth checking to see if a discount is available.

Adaptations to vehicles

A car may need to be adapted to suit the needs of a disabled person. The Department of Environment, Transport and the Regions Mobility Advice and Vehicle Information Service (MAVIS) offers advice on car adaptations for drivers and passengers.

Exemption from road tax

Any vehicle which is used only for a disabled person (whether they are the driver or the passenger) will be exempt from road tax. To get exemption, the disabled person must be either:
⇨ receiving the higher rate mobility component of disability living allowance; or
⇨ receiving a war pensioners' mobility supplement.

The vehicle must be registered in the name of the disabled person or in the name of someone authorised to act on their behalf.

Parking concessions

The blue badge scheme (this scheme used to be called the orange badge scheme) allows certain groups of disabled people to park in parking restricted areas. For example, the blue badge enables disabled people to park free of charge and without time limit at on-street parking-meters. Some London boroughs and other town centres don't operate this scheme. You should check whether the scheme operates before parking with your blue badge. There is an online service called the Blue Badge parking map which can help you find blue badge parking bays in 64 towns and cities across the UK. You can find the map at: www.direct.gov.uk/bluebadgemap.

You are eligible to apply for a blue badge if you are a driver or passenger who:

⇨ receives the higher rate mobility component of disability living allowance or war pensioners' mobility supplement, or are registered blind;
⇨ has a permanent and substantial disability which means you are unable to walk or walk only with considerable difficulty;
⇨ has very severe upper limb disabilities (drivers only).

To apply for a blue badge in England and Wales, contact your local authority social services department. In Scotland, contact the chief executive or social work department of the local authority, and in Northern Ireland, the Department for Regional Development. There is a small fee.

> **Public transport operators have the same duties as any other service provider as far as disability discrimination is concerned**

If you have a blue badge you may be able to get parking concessions when travelling in another country that also recognises the badge. However, each country continues to determine its own set of parking concessions for which the badge can be used. There is further information on the Department for Transport website www.mobility-unit.dft.gov.uk. In Northern Ireland, you can find information on the Roads Service website at: www.roadsni.gov.uk/BlueBadge/bbadge.htm.

Public transport

Public transport operators have the same duties as any other service provider as far as disability discrimination is concerned. This means they mustn't treat you less favourably than they would treat a person who isn't disabled, unless they can show that the treatment is justified. This applies to the vehicle itself as well as to other services provided by the operator, such as timetable information or facilities at a station. Aeroplanes and ships are not covered by these rules but the other services provided by aircraft and shipping companies are covered.

Rail services

All station and train operators must have a disabled people's protection policy which is approved by the Rail Regulator. The policy will set out what provision a station or train operator makes for disabled people using its services. Information on these services and a copy of the protection policy is available from the local train or station operator. Alternatively, most local authorities and Passenger Transport Executives publish guides for disabled travellers which are a useful source of information on the facilities at railway stations.

If you need assistance when travelling by train, for example, if you are a wheelchair user and need help getting on and off the train, or you are visually impaired and need to be guided to the train, contact the train operator and ask them to arrange assistance. Try to give the operator at least 48 hours' notice of when you intend to travel and the type of help you require. Most mainline stations have a staff member who deals with requests for assistance. That person will be able to make any arrangements needed with other operating companies.

In Northern Ireland, the Disability Discrimination Act allows the Northern Ireland Department of the Environment to ensure that all trains brought into use after 31 December 1998 operated by Northern Ireland Railways are accessible to disabled people.

Concessionary fares

If you are disabled you can buy a disabled person's railcard which entitles you and an accompanying adult to one-third off the price of a rail ticket. Application forms are available from main stations, or from the Disabled Person's Railcard Office. Existing railcard users can renew their railcard by telephone.

In Northern Ireland, disabled people aged 16-65 can travel for half price on trains (after 65 you can travel for free). You will need to apply to the Concessionary Fare Scheme for a half-fare smart-pass.

Complaints

If you are not satisfied with any arrangements made or any aspect of accessibility complain to the train operator. If the operator has not kept to the terms of its disabled person's protection policy, a complaint should be made to the Office of the Rail Regulator.

Buses

Outside London, most Passenger Transport Authorities and local authorities with responsibility for public transport publish guides for disabled travellers. In London, a person with an enquiry about disability access to buses should contact Transport for London Access and Mobility.

In some areas there are Dial-a-bus schemes providing door-to-door services for disabled people. You can get information from the local authority social services department or a local organisation for disabled people.

There are regulations covering coaches and buses so that disabled people can get on and off in safety and reasonable comfort. These depend on when a bus was brought into service,

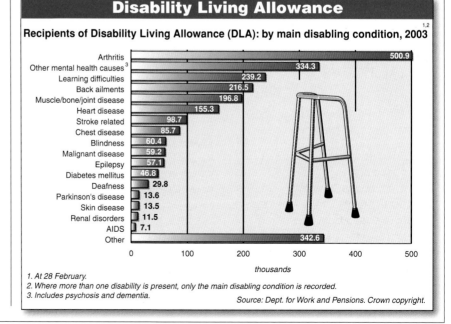

Disability Living Allowance

Recipients of Disability Living Allowance (DLA): by main disabling condition, 2003 [1,2]

Condition	thousands
Arthritis	500.9
Other mental health causes [3]	334.3
Learning difficulties	239.2
Back ailments	216.5
Muscle/bone/joint disease	196.8
Heart disease	155.3
Stroke related	98.7
Chest disease	85.7
Blindness	60.4
Malignant disease	59.2
Epilepsy	57.1
Diabetes mellitus	46.8
Deafness	29.8
Parkinson's disease	13.6
Skin disease	13.5
Renal disorders	11.5
AIDS	7.1
Other	342.6

1. At 28 February.
2. Where more than one disability is present, only the main disabling condition is recorded.
3. Includes psychosis and dementia.

Source: Dept. for Work and Pensions. Crown copyright.

but may include the need for ramps, steps and priority seating. A driver or conductor must help you get on or off of the bus if you ask, unless there are health and safety concerns about doing so.

Concessionary fares for disabled people in England, Wales and Scotland

In England, disabled people are entitled to free bus travel within the local authority area in which they live. In Wales and Scotland, disabled people and essential companions for disabled people are entitled to a free bus pass.

Concessionary fares for disabled people in Northern Ireland

In Northern Ireland, disabled people aged 16-65 can travel for half price on buses (after 65 you can travel for free). You will need to apply to the Concessionary Fare Scheme for a half-fare smart-pass.

Complaints

If you are dissatisfied with access to a bus service, complain to the bus operator. You may also want to draw the problem to the attention of the director of your local authority. The local authority may take up the complaint but will have no formal powers to make the operator respond.

Coaches

There are similar provisions for disability access to coaches as for buses (see above). If you plan to travel by coach you may want to contact the operator when arranging the journey to let the operator know what arrangements you need and to see whether the facilities exist to meet them.

Underground services

There are similar provisions for disability access to underground services as for coaches and buses – see above. To check provisions for disabled people on the underground service in your area, contact the Passenger Transport Executive (PTE) for travel outside London, or Transport for London's Access and Mobility for travel in London.

Disabled people may be entitled to concessionary fares on the underground.

Taxis and minicabs

Drivers of licensed taxis and minicabs are required to carry a guide dog and hearing dog, or an assistance dog accompanying a person with epilepsy or a physical disability, free of charge.

Under the Disability Discrimination Act, the government has the power to make regulations requiring all licensed taxis to be accessible to disabled people, including those who use wheelchairs, and to allow them to be carried in safety and reasonable comfort. Drivers of taxis which have been made accessible for disabled people will be obliged to help them in and out of their taxis and help with luggage.

In London, all newly-licensed taxis must be able to carry a wheelchair and all taxis must be wheelchair accessible by 1 January 2012.

Apart from the provision about dogs, mentioned earlier, there is no provision for disability access to minicabs.

Northern Ireland operates a public and private hire taxi service. Public hire (black) taxis display a yellow plate issued by the Department of the Environment and operate from ranks. They are required to carry guide and hearing dogs or assistance dogs as in Great Britain. They must also be wheelchair accessible. This is not the case with private hire taxis.

Aircraft

If you plan to travel by air you should inform your travel agent or the airline of your special needs and what kind of assistance you will need both in the airport and on the aircraft.

For example, wheelchairs may be available at large airports and it may be possible to arrange special seating on the aircraft. The airline can arrange for a porter to help with baggage and for someone to help you through immigration and customs controls.

Escort services and other help

Red Cross Escort Service

The Red Cross provides an escort service to enable disabled people make short or long journeys that they would otherwise find difficult. Escort services include providing a companion for a journey on public transport, a private car with a driver or a Red Cross ambulance. A charge is made.

St John Patient Transport Service in Wales

St John Cymru Wales can provide non-emergency medical transport for people who have difficulty in using public transport or normal cars. They can provide specially adapted wheelchair-accessible vehicles and fully equipped ambulances. They also provide a hospital car service for able-bodied patients, driven by drivers trained in emergency aid and manual handling. A charge is made for all these services. For more information, visit the St John Cymru Wales website at: www.stjohnwales.co.uk.

Thistle Travel Card Scheme (Scotland only)

The Thistle Travel Card scheme, in Scotland, helps people with a disability to use public transport. The card indicates to transport staff that its holder has a learning or other disability and may need support during their journey. The scheme applies to buses, trains (including underground trains) and taxis. The card does not give the holder a travel discount or concession. You can get the card in transport booking offices, local authority concessionary travel offices, day centres and carers' centres. The scheme is administered by Enable Scotland.

⇨ Information from www.adviceguide.org.uk at February 2007, the public information website for national charity Citizens' Advice.

© Citizens' Advice

Young carers

There are over 175,000 young people in the UK caring for someone with a physical or learning disability, illness or substance dependency

What is a young carer?

Young carers look after a relative or friend who needs support because of a physical or learning disability, illness or substance dependency. Caring is classed as everything from intensive support through to more simple tasks such as communicating for deaf relatives.

> **Many young people don't see themselves as carers or consider seeking help when they find it hard to cope with the situation**

What caring amounts to is a role reversal as these young people have to grow up and learn responsibility far more quickly. Many young people become carers for several years and some will be committed to caring for many years. This can bring feelings of intense isolation in the carer.

How many young carers exist?

The Department of Health had thought there were 32,000 young carers in the UK. The 2001 Census found 175,000. Some 13,000 are providing more than 50 hours of help a week. There are problems with the way these figures are constructed. The stats show 85% of all young carers provide 1-19 hours of care a week to a disabled, frail or chronically ill person. This lack of detail masks some important issues. There is a massive difference between caring for a disabled sibling for a couple of hours a week and being the sole carer for a single parent with severe mental illness. The impact of home situations can differ greatly from carer to carer.

Caring is also considered a hidden problem. Many young people don't see themselves as carers or consider seeking help when they find it hard to cope with the situation. Many younger carers of school age also fail to seek help when their situation makes them a target for bullies.

Help for young carers

Ewan Main, a support worker for the Princess Royal Trust for Young Carers, has some advice for young carers on how to cope with the situation:

⇨ It's very important to take time away from the situation: It may be hard to get some time away from the person you are caring for. But it's important to try and do some of the things that give you pleasure. You may want to play a sport, relax with friends or listen to music;

⇨ If it's possible try and share the care: Caring for someone can leave you worn out. To stop yourself from becoming run down, it may be helpful to share caring responsibility with someone else;

⇨ Get in touch with some support groups: When you are caring for someone you may sometimes feel you're the only person in the world in that situation. Friends may not understand your life. Talking to people who are in a similar situation may be helpful. You may be able to do this by taking part in activities for young carers;

⇨ Learn about the illness/disability/substance dependency of the person you are caring for: Knowing about the illness/disability may be helpful in understanding your relative's behaviour or moods. If you are giving medication it is a good idea to know about the illness/disability;

⇨ Most important of all, talk to someone: It is normal for you to go through phases when you are feeling angry, frustrated, guilty, sad, scared or worried. During those times it may be helpful to talk to someone you trust about how you are feeling. Friends, other carers, and family are people who might be helpful to speak with. If these feelings are stopping you from doing day-to-day things it may be helpful to see someone, like a counsellor.

⇨ The above information is reprinted with kind permission from TheSite.org. Visit www.thesite.org for more information.

© TheSite.org

'Hidden Lives'

New report shows reality of life for children caring behind closed doors

A new report and YouGov survey published today by Barnardo's indicates that children caring for parents with addictions, mental health issues or physical disabilities are missing out on vital support.

Barnardo's provides services for young carers across the UK and we have long suspected that many of them are failing to be identified by schools, social services or young carer support projects and that many have to wait years to find help. The official figure for young carers* in the UK is 175,000 but we fear that this is a marked underestimate.

The official figure for young carers in the UK is 175,000 but we fear that this is a marked underestimate

---

The new report *Hidden Lives* (available as PDF) has exposed the fact that many young carers are not captured in official statistics and are effectively left to cope alone, often for years. It includes a YouGov poll of 1,000 primary and secondary school teachers. We have discovered that:
⇨ 91% of teachers believe that some young carers are falling through the net and remaining unidentified.
⇨ 78% of teachers surveyed believed that the families of young carers (who do not request support) have deliberately taken the decision not to inform social services for fear that the department might get involved in an unwelcome way (for example by breaking the family up).
⇨ Around three-quarters of teachers thought young carers hide their situation from teachers (72%) and other school children (75%).
⇨ 50% of teachers thought that the system in schools supposedly

Barnardo's
GIVING CHILDREN BACK THEIR FUTURE

designed to identify and support young carers was not effective enough.

We have also compiled a survey asking 83 children from Barnardo's young carers' projects about the reality of their lives. This revealed that:
⇨ on average each young carer had spent a total of four years looking after a parent or relative before they received any support.
⇨ most young carers were aged 13-15 years and had caring duties that lasted on average 17 hours a week.

Both surveys drew attention to a 'culture of secrecy' that exists amongst both young carers and their families.

'At least 175,000 children and young people are forced to give up their childhoods so that they can care for a parent, brother or sister who is seriously ill. They have huge responsibilities that most adults never

have to face, some providing care for 30 hours or more a week.* They often have to administer medicines, bath parents, pay bills, and be responsible for shopping for the family; as well as looking after younger brothers and sisters. Without support, they can miss out on childhood altogether,' said Martin Narey, Barnardo's Chief Executive.

To coincide with the publication of the survey, Barnardo's is launching (on 7 November) a new radio and magazine advertising campaign to highlight the problem. We are looking for 175,000 people to sign up to the latest campaign to give their 'permission' for young carers to have a break. For more information please log on to www.barnardos.org.uk

All findings and recommendations are listed in the new Barnardo's report: *Hidden Lives – unidentified young carers in the UK* (1.8 Mb pdf).
* *UK 2001 Census of Population, Office of National Statistics, London.*
6 November 2006

⇨ The above information is re-printed with kind permission from Barnardo's. To view the full report, go to http://www.barnardos.org.uk/hidden_lives_report-2.pdf
© *Barnardo's*

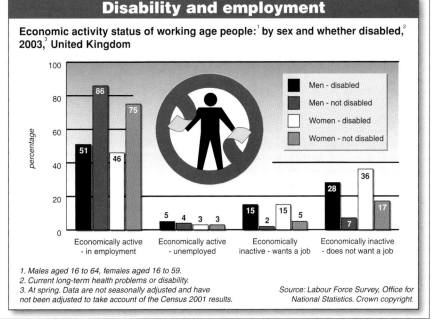

Disability and employment

Economic activity status of working age people:[1] by sex and whether disabled,[2] 2003,[3] United Kingdom

Legend:
- Men - disabled
- Men - not disabled
- Women - disabled
- Women - not disabled

percentage

Economically active - in employment: 51, 86, 46, 75
Economically active - unemployed: 5, 4, 3, 3
Economically inactive - wants a job: 15, 2, 15, 5
Economically inactive - does not want a job: 28, 7, 36, 17

1. Males aged 16 to 64, females aged 16 to 59.
2. Current long-term health problems or disability.
3. At spring. Data are not seasonally adjusted and have not been adjusted to take account of the Census 2001 results.

Source: Labour Force Survey, Office for National Statistics. Crown copyright.

Ross's story

Ross, 17, helps to look after one of his brothers who has a learning disability

Ross's brother is 13, but has a mental age of three or four. He was born with a chromosome abnormality, which means he has severe learning difficulties and problems with his behaviour.

He has a form of autism and ADHD (Attention Deficit Hyperactivity Disorder).

> **'Ever since I was old enough I have been helping out with my brother, mainly by playing with him, feeding him and helping him get dressed'**

Ross lives at home with his parents, his three brothers and his sister, who are aged between seven and 14.

Helping out

Ever since I was old enough I have been helping out with my brother, mainly by playing with him, feeding him and helping him get dressed. I also look after him when our parents go out.

It is like looking after a three- or four-year-old. He can't talk, read or

www.youngcarers.net

write, but he makes noises, which I can understand a bit.

How it affects us

It is very difficult for the family to carry out everyday tasks like shopping. We hardly ever go out and haven't been on holiday for several years.

The most stressful part to deal with is his behaviour. He is 'slap happy', pulls hair and is very hyperactive. Sometimes he can be very obnoxious. He often wakes up really early in the mornings, which generally means that the rest of the family wakes up early too.

Looking after my brother has changed my personality in some ways – I have had to become more responsible.

Dealing with it

I don't go out much, but I like to relax by sitting and listening to music in my room.

Usually I just bob along and try to keep calm, but sometimes I get fed up and deal with this by shouting and screaming and storming off somewhere. I don't really talk about it much to my friends, so I'm not sure what they know about it.

For one night every two weeks my brother is taken away to be cared for by someone else, to give us a break. This helps, but it is only for one night and so we never have a full weekend free. One thing that would really make a difference would be to have some more free time.

The future

Recently I left school. I never had any problems there, except for tiredness, but I didn't enjoy it. For the last three months I have been working as an apprentice painter, which is going really well.

As a family we have all talked about what is going to happen to my brother in the future and how we will look after him. We have all agreed to share the burden as our parents get older. We can't put him in a home, as it wouldn't be fair on him.

⇨ Information from the Princess Royal Trust for Carers. Please visit their website at www.youngcarers. net or www.carers.org for more information.

© Princess Royal Trust for Carers

Equality rights

Equality rights for disabled people finally go public

From today (4 December), a new duty imposed by the Disability Discrimination Act 2005 forces the public sector to take the needs of disabled people into account when planning everything from transport to websites.

'Public services must be planned and designed with disabled people in mind'

The Disability Equality Duty (DED) places public bodies under a legal obligation to 'mainstream' disabled people when planning services. In carrying out their functions, the Act says public authorities must 'have due regard' to disabled people's needs; it is not enough for public bodies to act in a non-discriminatory way; they must now actively promote equality for people with disabilities, and a positive attitude to them.

To comply with the duty, public authorities must:

⇨ promote equality of opportunity between disabled persons and other persons

⇨ eliminate discrimination that is unlawful under the Act

⇨ eliminate harassment of disabled persons related to their disabilities

⇨ encourage participation by disabled persons in public life

⇨ take steps to take account of disabled persons' disabilities, even where that involves treating disabled persons more favourably than other persons.

The Disability Equality Duty (DED) covers all of the 45,000-odd organisations in the public

ARTHRITIS CARE
Empowering people with arthritis.

sector – including those involved in the making of policy and those delivering services, like transport, to the public.

Under the new duty, people employed in the public sector must consider the effect of their policy and practices on disabled people, and act to eliminate any disability inequality. This should mean fairer and better employment opportunities for disabled people, and freedom from discrimination, negative attitudes, or harassment when using a service.

'Public services must be planned and designed with disabled people in mind. Libraries, swimming pools, hospitals, local public transport, you name it, they must be planned with, and for, disabled people just as much as for other people.

'It means the onus is no longer on the individual to complain if they have experienced problems or discrimination, it is for the public body to anticipate potential inequality

and head it off before it happens,' said Rachel Haynes, Arthritis Care's director of public affairs.

'The public bodies also have to report on how they are implementing the duty, and how they have involved disabled people in their planning. And whilst the new duty does not create new individual rights for disabled people, it does mean a public body which fails to comply with the duty may expose itself to judicial review of its action or inaction,' said Ms Haynes.

4 December 2006

⇨ Arthritis Care is the UK's largest voluntary organisation working with and for all people with arthritis. It provides information and support on a range of issues related to living with arthritis. Arthritis Care campaigns locally and nationally to make sure people with arthritis have access to the treatments and services they deserve. Call Arthritis Care's freephone confidential helpline service on 0808 800 4050 from 10am to 4pm Monday to Friday or email helplines@ arthritiscare.org.uk. Visit the website at www.arthritiscare.org.uk

© *Arthritis Care*

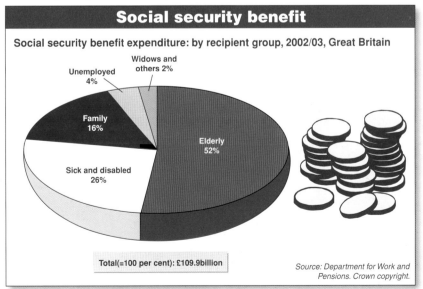

Social security benefit

Social security benefit expenditure: by recipient group, 2002/03, Great Britain

- Widows and others 2%
- Unemployed 4%
- Family 16%
- Elderly 52%
- Sick and disabled 26%

Total(=100 per cent): £109.9billion

Source: Department for Work and Pensions. Crown copyright.

The disability symbol

Information from the Employers' Forum on Disability

The disability symbol, which is a Government initiative, has been developed so employers can show their commitment to good practice in employing disabled people. It is a communication tool which can be used by employers to encourage disabled people to apply for specific jobs. Employers who use the symbol make five commitments to action.

These are :

⇨ A guaranteed job interview: To interview all applicants with a disability who meet the minimum criteria for a job vacancy and to consider them on their abilities.

⇨ Consulting disabled employees regularly: To ask disabled employees at least once a year what you can do to make sure they can develop and use their abilities at work.

Symbol users are expected to put the symbol on all job advertisements in the press or at the Jobcentre

⇨ Keeping employees if they become disabled: To make every effort when employees become disabled to make sure they stay in employment.

⇨ Improving knowledge: To take action to ensure that key employees develop the awareness of disability needed to make your commitments.

⇨ Checking progress and planning ahead: Each year, to review these commitments and what has been achieved, plan ways to improve on them and let all your employees know about progress and future plans.

Symbol users are expected to put the symbol on all job advertisements in the press or at the Jobcentre, as well as internal vacancy advertisements

The disability symbol. The symbol allows employers to show their commitment to good practice in employing disabled people

and job application forms. The symbol can also be put on letterheads and stationery; internal magazines and newsletters; doorways and signs in personnel departments, reception areas, interview rooms and at career exhibitions.

The symbol was launched prior to the Disability Discrimination Act and work that an employer does to implement the five symbol commitments would certainly contribute to working to the spirit of that legislation. It is important to recognise, however, that using the disability symbol does not in itself mean an organisation will meet the requirements of the Disability Discrimination Act. If you have any concerns about how the Disability Discrimination Act impacts on your organisation, you should contact your legal advisers.

⇨ The above information is re-printed with kind permission from the Employers' Forum on Disability. Visit www.employers-forum.co.uk for more information.

© Employers' Forum on Disability

Diversity good for business

Information from *Disability Now*

Businesses with a diverse workforce attract more business, according to new research.

The Jobcentre Plus research revealed that more than half of customers would be more likely to use a business that employed people who were disabled, older, or from ethnic minorities.

Four-fifths of respondents felt the existence of a diversity policy in businesses was important.

Chief executive of Jobcentre Plus, Lesley Strathie, said: 'This research proves to employers that being committed to diversity is not a business choice, but a business imperative.

'Customers and employees want to shop and work in environments which reflect their local communities.'

Nick Bason, information and policy manager at the Employers' Forum on Disability, said: 'There are commercial, professional and strategic benefits for a company in employing a diverse workforce.

'A company that can understand difference is much more likely to be able to understand the diverse needs of their customers...being confident in engaging with diversity is not only the right thing to do, it can give a significant commercial advantage.'

Over half (58 per cent) of employers claimed to already employ a varied workforce, with 100,000 disabled people starting work last year through Jobcentre Plus.

February 2007

⇨ Information from *Disability Now* (www.disabilitynow.org.uk). To subscribe to *Disability Now* and for a free sample copy, contact: 0845 130 9177, email: dnsubs@servicehelpline.co.uk

© *Disability Now*

Workplace prejudice

A third of disabled workers have experienced workplace prejudice

IT training and flexible working key to creating a level playing field. New research from Leonard Cheshire and Microsoft has revealed that almost a third (30%) of disabled people have experienced prejudice in the workplace and 28% of business managers think employers are reluctant to employ disabled people because of other people's attitudes.

The survey of small and medium-sized businesses and members of Leonard Cheshire's Disabled People's Forum, which replicates similar research conducted by the two organisations in 2002, reveals that although business managers now have a better awareness of policy and guidelines relating to the employment of disabled workers, there is by no means a level playing field.

According to the Disability Rights Commission, only 50% of the 6.8 million disabled people of working age in Britain are in employment

According to the Disability Rights Commission, only 50% of the 6.8 million disabled people of working age in Britain are in employment, compared to 81% of non-disabled people, and a massive one million disabled people without a job want to work.

The two main reasons cited by the managers questioned explaining why they didn't have disabled people on the payroll, were that 'opportunities had not yet arisen' (by 47%) and 'the type of work was unsuitable' (by 17%). Worryingly, nearly three in 10 (29%) of the managers questioned were unaware of the policy and guidelines relating to the employment of disabled workers at their company, although this figure is an improvement on the 44% who were unaware in 2002.

According to those questioned from Leonard Cheshire's Disabled People's Forum, the most important factor required to address these workplace inequalities is better training and education for disabled people. Indeed respondents considered this more important than 'changing employers' attitudes to disabled workers' and the creation of 'more legislation to ensure disabled workers' rights are met'.

Having the right support systems and equipment was also considered vital. A massive 90% of respondents said it was important to have the right IT training to perform their job, 76% said it was important to have the right equipment and software and 63% mentioned the importance of working flexibly.

Clare Evans, Head of Service User Support at Leonard Cheshire, said: 'Employers need to be more flexible about their approach to employing disabled people so that they can benefit from the skills of the 1 million disabled people looking for work.

'Making the workplace more accessible is not purely about physical alterations. This survey highlights that the right training, software and particularly attitudes are equally important and these types of modification are not only simple, but relatively low cost and easy to implement in the workplace.'

Leonard Cheshire and Microsoft have worked together for nine years on an initiative called Workability, which aims to equip disabled people who are seeking employment with ICT skills necessary for the workplace. The scheme also engages with employers to arrange work placements, provide careers advice and to secure employment opportunities for participants. Since 1997, Workability has supported almost 4,000 disabled people, with 1,750 going on to further education or into employment.

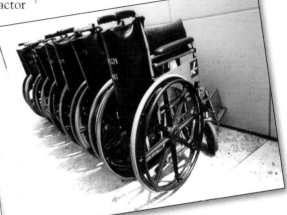

Microsoft's Head of Citizenship Bronwyn Kunhardt commented: 'It's worrying that such a large percentage of the population aren't able to fulfil their potential in the workplace, because they don't have access to the right training and because of the uphill struggle they face to overcome prejudice.

'There is no question that proper training, accessible technology and flexible working all play a vitally important part in creating equal opportunities, and that's why schemes such as Workability are so important.'

28 August 2006

⇨ The above information is re-printed with kind permission from Leonard Cheshire. Visit www.leonard-cheshire.org for more information.

Disabled people continue to bear brunt of UK poverty

Information from the Disability Rights Commission

The song remains the same for disabled people and people with long-term health conditions the Disability Rights Commission (DRC) said today, after publication of the latest figures monitoring the success of Government policies aimed at reducing poverty.

Commenting on figures compiled by the New Policy Institute for the Joseph Rowntree Trust, the Commission underlined its call for policies aimed at supporting whole families out of poverty, rather than benefits targeting individuals as the only means to bring about an alternative future for the thousands of disabled people living in poverty.

'At 30%, the poverty rate for disabled adults is twice that for non disabled adults'

With 'worklessness' being pinpointed as a key driver behind increased levels of poverty among disabled people, the Commission also pinpointed the forthcoming Leitch Review into skills as being a key moment to view the Government's real intent in tackling the barriers to participation that disabled people face entering the labour market.

A spokesperson for the DRC said:

'The song remains the same for disabled people and people with long-term health conditions living in poverty today. At 30%, the poverty rate for disabled adults is twice that for non-disabled adults. The gap between them is higher now than a decade ago. And traditional routes out of poverty through work are also barred – a disabled graduate is more likely to be out of work than a non-disabled person without qualifications and one-quarter of disabled parents in poverty are already in jobs. Any serious observer of persistent poverty in Britain today knows that it frequently has disadvantage related to disability at its root. Tackling poverty effectively means putting disability at the heart of the solution.'

The DRC's Disability Agenda to be launched in February provides the means for the link between disability and poverty to be broken and for child poverty to be eliminated by 2020.

A spokesperson said:

'Ending poverty, including child poverty, demands reforms to the welfare state that focus help onto the family as a whole, not just separately onto individuals. Services should help families take control of their own lives, escape dependency and build resilience against poverty as well as optimise their potential to achieve economic well-being.'

4 December 2006

⇨ The above information is reprinted with kind permission from the Disability Rights Commission. Visit www.drc-gb.org for more.

© *Disability Rights Commission*

Disability and employment statistics

Information from the Shaw Trust

The following is according to the UK's Office for National Statistics' *Labour Force Survey*, Spring 2005, for people of working age only.

⇨ Nearly one in five people of working age (7 million, or 19%) in Great Britain are disabled.

⇨ There has been an increase in the number of working-age people reporting a disability; from 6.2 million in Spring 1998 to 7 million in Spring 2005.

⇨ Only about half of disabled people of working age are in work (50%), compared with 80% of non-disabled people of working age.

⇨ Almost half (46%) of the disabled population of working age in Britain are economically inactive i.e. outside of the labour force. Only 16% of non-disabled people of working age are economically inactive.

⇨ Nearly one-third of disabled people who are economically inactive say they would like to work (28%), compared with less than one-quarter (24%) of non-disabled economically inactive people.

⇨ Employment rates vary greatly according to the type of impairment a person has. Disabled people with mental health problems have the lowest employment rates of all impairment categories at only 20%.

⇨ Disabled people are more than twice as likely as non-disabled people to have no qualifications (26% as opposed to 11%).

⇨ The above information is reprinted with kind permission from the Shaw Trust. Visit www.shaw-trust.org.uk for more information.

© *Shaw Trust*

The cost of poverty

Disabled people are hit harder by poverty than any other group, but Paul Treloar, director of policy and services at the charity Disability Alliance, says the government has yet to act

It can be an expensive business being poor. You probably pay more for your gas and electricity, you can only access credit with extortionate rates of interest and if you find work and get a pay rise, this is wiped out through the loss of housing and council tax benefit at a rate of 85p for every extra pound earned.

There are now more disabled adults living in poverty than either children or pensioners. Add in the extra costs related to disability, and it isn't difficult to see why enduring poverty for disabled people is one of the key challenges yet to be addressed by government initiatives to reduce poverty and combat social exclusion.

The most recent income poverty estimates suggest that 27 per cent of working-age households with at least one disabled adult are on the lowest incomes. This compares to 16 per cent of households with no disabled adult.

Notwithstanding this disparity, these statistics do not measure the disability-related extra costs incurred by disabled people, when comparing their needs to those of non-disabled people. If these extra costs were factored in, up to 60 per cent of disabled people might be living in poverty.

Disability alliance

Recent research found that disabled people solely reliant on benefits have an approximate shortfall of £200 per week in the figure required to ensure a minimum standard of living. This figure is irrespective of the type or level of their need and assumes maximum take-up of benefits and no personal assistance costs.

A disabled person in work could have a shortfall of £118 to £189 per week, even if full housing and council tax benefit is being paid, but many people even in low-paid work are unlikely to receive these full benefits, so the net shortfall could be even higher.

Disabled people have a wide range of additional costs, from personal assistance and transport to housing, household goods, laundry, clothing and footwear. These costs can arise as the direct effect of a person's particular impairment, for example, wheelchairs, incontinence pads or bathroom adaptations.

Some of these should be provided by statutory services but delays and patchy local provision often mean that disabled people end up paying for items themselves.

There are also costs arising from environmental issues or as a result of discrimination, for example, inaccessible public transport and venues, a lack of sign language provision, as well as more direct discrimination such as extra premiums for life assurance or lower wages than non-disabled workers of equivalent status.

And all of these additional costs can be on top of problems that potentially affect all people living in poverty: higher costs for gas and electricity, susceptibility to debt, inability to make savings, poor diet and health, spending more on housing costs while often living in substandard accommodation, lack of access to services, and social isolation and exclusion.

The government mantra, 'work is the best route out of poverty', may be true for some people, but it overlooks many startling figures.

Research suggests that disabled people receive wages that are, on average, 20 per cent lower than for other employees. The research also found evidence of a lack of training or promotion opportunities for disabled people.

Even getting a job can be difficult when six out of ten employers would not consider employing someone diagnosed with a mental health problem. Four times as many adults with a work-limiting disability are currently out of work, compared with their non-disabled counterparts.

If disabled people are to be lifted out of poverty, there are at least four key changes required.

The first, and most obvious, is to deal with the inadequacy and low take-up

of benefits and tax credits. Significant investment is needed to ensure that disability-related extra costs are reflected in levels of incapacity and disability benefits, as opposed to the threat of benefit sanctions proposed in the welfare reform bill.

Second, the additional costs faced by disabled people need to be recognised, measured and factored into any poverty statistics.

Third, provision of statutory and non-statutory support services requires major improvement. Patchy provision and difficulties in accessing services can lead to greater expense and increase the threat of falling into debt, as well as bringing about an increased risk of isolation and social exclusion.

Fourth, the Disability Discrimination Act and disability equality duty must be more widely publicised, monitored and enforced, especially in relation to low pay and employment.

Unless disabled people feel able to challenge discriminatory practices whenever they come across them, many of these challenges will endure, thus maintaining the unacceptable levels of poverty faced by many disabled people today.
January 2007

⇨ Information from the Disability Alliance. Visit www. disabilityalliance.org for more information. Please see also www. disabilityalliance.org/start.htm for more details on *Starting Out*, a guide about young people and benefits.
© *Paul Treloar/Disability Alliance*

Social care

General public's high expectations of adult social care

Ipsos MORI's recent research conducted on behalf of Disability Rights Commission (DRC) looks at public attitudes towards social care. The survey reveals that there is a gulf between expectation and provision of adult social care in Great Britain.

People feel that if they become disabled or develop a long-term health condition they would like to be able to make decisions about their own lives (81%)

Some of the key findings from the report are:
⇨ When asked about the likelihood of being able to provide regular unpaid care to a family member or friend who is disabled or has a long-term health condition, only one in five (21%) said they were very likely; while three in ten (29%) said they were fairly likely. However, more than a third of respondents (35%) said they were unlikely to provide regular unpaid care in the future.
⇨ People feel that if they become disabled or develop a long-term health condition they would like to be able to make decisions about their own lives (81%) and get support from Local Authorities to stay in their own house (57%).
⇨ Furthermore, the public would like social services or public agencies to provide support for them to stay in their own home (90%), provide basic needs such as food, shelter and medical care (88%) and give them the choice to not live in a residential care home (87%).
⇨ Half of the public stated that the cost of caring should be paid for by the individual, their close family or friends. On the other hand, a third of the public (32%) said that there should be no contribution towards the cost of caring.
⇨ Half of the public supports an increase in tax in order to fund better adult social care; however, a quarter of the public (26%) opposes an increase in tax. A quarter of the public (24%) remains undecided about whether they support or oppose a tax increase for better adult social care.

Technical details
Ipsos MORI interviewed a nationally representative quota sample of 2,053 adults aged 15+ in 202 sample points throughout Great Britain. Interviews were carried out face to face in respondents' homes. Fieldwork was conducted between 25-30 May 2006.
13 July 2006

⇨ The above information is reprinted with kind permission from Ipsos MORI. Visit www.ipsos-mori. com for more information.
© *Ipsos MORI*

Expectations of adult social care

Ipsos MORI interviewed a nationally representative quota sample of 2,053 adults aged 15+ in 202 sample points throughout Great Britain. Interviews were carried out face to face in respondents' homes. Fieldwork was conducted between 25-30 May 2006.

Are you or have you ever personally been responsible for providing care for any older or working-age relatives or friends who are disabled or have a long-term health condition? By care, we mean personal care like helping with washing, dressing, feeding, housework, shopping, going out etc. Which of the following categories applies to them?

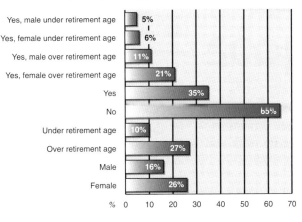

	%
Yes, male under retirement age	5%
Yes, female under retirement age	6%
Yes, male over retirement age	11%
Yes, female over retirement age	21%
Yes	35%
No	65%
Under retirement age	10%
Over retirement age	27%
Male	16%
Female	26%

How likely, if at all, is it that you would be able to provide regular unpaid care in the future, if a close relative or friend became disabled or developed a long-term health condition? Again, by care, we mean personal care like help with washing, dressing, feeding, housework, shopping, going out etc.

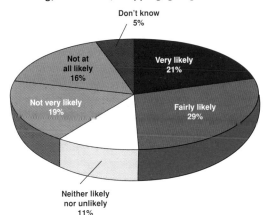

- Don't know 5%
- Not at all likely 16%
- Very likely 21%
- Not very likely 19%
- Fairly likely 29%
- Neither likely nor unlikely 11%

If you were to become disabled or develop a long-term health condition in the future, how likely do you believe it would be that you would . . .?

Legend: Very likely, Fairly likely, Neither likely nor unlikely, Not very likely, Not at all likely, Don't know

	Very likely	Fairly likely	Neither likely nor unlikely	Not very likely	Not at all likely	Don't know
Make decisions about your own life	47%	35%	8%	3	2%	6%
Have someone else make decisions about some aspects of your life	8%	37%	15%	20%	14%	6%
Move into a residential care home	5%	22%	18%	27%	20%	8%
Get support from your local authority to stay in your own home	21%	36%	14%	15%	5%	9%
Move in with (a) male family member(s)	5%	16%	15%	27%	30%	7%
Move in with (a) female family member(s)	9%	22%	14%	23%	25%	7%
Move in with male and female family members	8%	21%	15%	24%	25%	7%

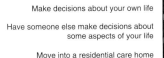

How much, if any, of the cost of caring for adults who are disabled or have long-term health conditions do you think should be paid for by the individual, their close family (spouse/partner, children, siblings) or friends? By costs, I mean costs of transport, clothing, toiletries, medicine and special food (excluding personal care and housing costs).

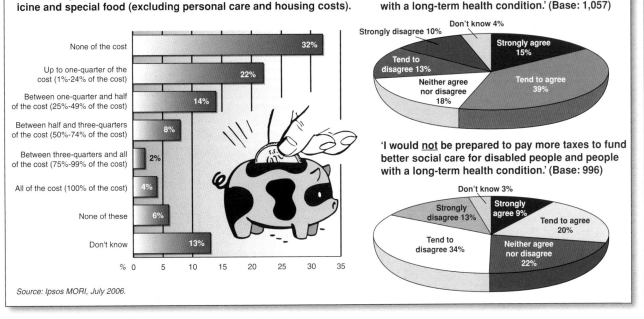

	%
None of the cost	32%
Up to one-quarter of the cost (1%-24% of the cost)	22%
Between one-quarter and half of the cost (25%-49% of the cost)	14%
Between half and three-quarters of the cost (50%-74% of the cost)	8%
Between three-quarters and all of the cost (75%-99% of the cost)	2%
All of the cost (100% of the cost)	4%
None of these	6%
Don't know	13%

To what extent, if at all, do you agree or disagree with the following statements?
'I would be prepared to pay more taxes to fund better social care for disabled people and people with a long-term health condition.' (Base: 1,057)

- Don't know 4%
- Strongly disagree 10%
- Strongly agree 15%
- Tend to disagree 13%
- Tend to agree 39%
- Neither agree nor disagree 18%

'I would not be prepared to pay more taxes to fund better social care for disabled people and people with a long-term health condition.' (Base: 996)

- Don't know 3%
- Strongly disagree 13%
- Strongly agree 9%
- Tend to disagree 34%
- Tend to agree 20%
- Neither agree nor disagree 22%

Source: Ipsos MORI, July 2006.

The Disability Discrimination Act (DDA)

Find out about the legislation that is in place to promote civil rights for disabled people and protect disabled people from discrimination

Disability rights in everyday life

This article is mainly about the Disability Discrimination Act itself. You can find out about your rights in different areas of life, including accessing and using the services of shops, cafes and banks – plus your rights in employment, health and education – from www.direct.gov.uk/en/DisabledPeople

The Disability Discrimination Act 1995 (DDA 1995)

The Disability Discrimination Act (DDA) 1995 aims to end the discrimination that many disabled people face. This Act gives disabled people rights in the areas of:
⇨ employment
⇨ education
⇨ access to goods, facilities and services
⇨ buying or renting land or property.

The Act also allows the government to set minimum standards so that disabled people can use public transport easily.

The Disability Discrimination Act 2005 (DDA 2005)

In April 2005 a new Disability Discrimination Act was passed by Parliament, which amends or extends existing provisions in the DDA 1995, including:
⇨ making it unlawful for operators of transport vehicles to discriminate against disabled people
⇨ making it easier for disabled people to rent property and for tenants to make disability-related adaptations
⇨ making sure that private clubs with 25 or more members cannot keep disabled people out, just because they have a disability
⇨ extending protection to cover people who have HIV, cancer and multiple sclerosis from the moment they are diagnosed
⇨ ensuring that discrimination law covers all the activities of the public sector
⇨ requiring public bodies to promote equality of opportunity for disabled people.

The Disability Discrimination Act (DDA) 1995 aims to end the discrimination that many disabled people face

---

Some of the new laws – including the increased protection for people who have HIV, cancer and multiple sclerosis – came into force in December 2005. The Department for Work and Pensions (DWP) website has more about the December 2005 changes.

Others changes came into force in December 2006 – the

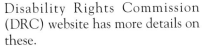

Disability Rights Commission (DRC) website has more details on these.

The DRC was set up by the government to help secure civil rights for disabled people and produces guidance and further information on which aspects of life are covered by anti-discrimination law for disabled people.

Changes to the Disability Discrimination Act (DDA 1995) in October 2004

The development of legislation to improve the rights of disabled people is an ongoing process. From 1 October 2004, Part 3 of the DDA 1995 has required businesses and other organisations to take reasonable steps to tackle physical features that act as a barrier to disabled people who want to access their services.

This may mean to remove, alter or provide a reasonable means of avoiding physical features of a building which make access impossible or unreasonably difficult for disabled people. Examples include:
⇨ putting in a ramp to replace steps
⇨ providing larger, well-defined signs for people with a visual impairment
⇨ improving access to toilet or washing facilities.

Businesses and organisations are called 'service providers' and include shops, restaurants, leisure centres and places of worship.

⇨ The above information is reprinted with kind permission from Directgov. Visit www.direct.gov.uk for more information.
© Crown copyright

The campaign for real choice

A year after the extension of the Disability Discrimination Act, Ben Furner looks at what has been achieved since, and what remains to be done to improve the lives of disabled people

The passing of another International Day of Disabled Persons marks another year of highs and lows for disabled people in the UK. Changes to the law and new government policy and initiatives have been welcomed by campaigners. But anxieties about welfare reform, funding for social care and independent living and the debate around 'right to die' legislation continue to be at the forefront of the disability movement's mind.

Anxieties about welfare reform, funding for social care and independent living and the debate around 'right to die' legislation continue to be at the forefront of the disability movement's mind

---

The minister for disabled people, Anne McGuire, is quick to try to allay fears and lists the progress that has been made: establishment of the Office for Disability Issues (ODI), which monitors and co-ordinates policy development for disability issues across government departments; changes to disability discrimination legislation; and new requirements on public authorities to promote disability equality, which came into force this week. The changes send a strong message that disabled people will welcome and come alongside new legal protection for people with cancer, multiple sclerosis and HIV.

Lisa Power, head of policy at HIV/Aids charity the Terrence Higgins Trust, says changes in legislation so far have allowed those living with HIV to be more open about their diagnosis. 'People with HIV deserve a fair deal and the Disability Discrimination Act is helping to ensure they get it.'

And disabled people are pleased that some of their other concerns appear to have been taken on board. The welfare reform bill, currently in committee stage in Parliament, has seen a concerted lobbying effort by disabled people, with some concessions being made. While the devil may be in the detail, McGuire is clear about the government's approach: 'The reforms are not about forcing people off benefits, nor about forcing people into jobs.'

The growth of direct payments is also cause for celebration, alongside pilot schemes for individual budgets which give disabled people more independence.

Mental health issues have become more central, with some intensive lobbying work by mental health charities on government plans to revamp legislation in that area. In the autumn there was a flurry of activity around World Mental Health Day, including the launch of the government-backed Action on Stigma campaign. A number of public figures spoke openly about their personal experiences of mental illness.

Many of the changes made or in progress need to be considered in the light of *Improving the Life Chances of Disabled People*, the report published by the prime minister's strategy unit nearly two years ago. The report, which was broadly welcomed by disabled people, made more than 60 recommendations for government departments to consider.

Bert Massie, chair of the Disability Rights Commission (DRC), believes the report has already made a difference now that families with disabled children no longer face a means test to get grants for adapting the family home, and it has helped 'push disability up the agenda'.

He, and many others, are now looking to the ODI to ensure the recommendations are followed up. It has been busy in its first year, but there's more to come, says Jos Joures, the ODI's assistant director. 'The

'Institutional disablism' is rife in Britain

Information from Demos

'Institutional disablism' is rife in the UK, according to a report published by Demos and Scope. *Disablist Britain: Barriers to independent living for disabled people in 2006* documents for the first time the extent of systemic discrimination towards disabled people in the UK across employment, housing and social care, transport, leisure and status. The report was commissioned by disability organisation Scope in partnership with Disability Awareness in Action.

The report was launched on 9th March 2006 by John Hutton MP, Secretary of State for Work and Pensions, at a Disablism Summit organised by Scope.

'The issues addressed in today's conference clearly set out the challenge we still face in creating an equal society', said John Hutton MP. 'It is vital that we collect evidence about the life chances of disabled people and that is why the Government's new Office for Disability Issues is working with disabled people and their representative organisations on ways of measuring progress towards our goal of a fully inclusive Britain.'

The report draws upon statistical data from the largest number of sources yet committed to one volume on the subject, including government statistics, census figures and not-for-profit and think-tank polling, to outline disabled people's experiences of British state and society.

'Disablism runs wild in our society because the evidence illustrating how disabled people are treated is rarely publicised or collated,' says Tony Manwaring, Chief Executive of Scope. 'Disablist Britain shows that whatever stone one upturns in this country, disablism lies beneath. We must find it and stomp it out. Only then will disabled people have the right, in practice, to make the same choices as non-disabled people to live the lives they choose.'

Demos and the disability partners behind the report hope that the audit will contribute towards the creation of a benchmark against which to measure, identify and eradicate disablism. The validity and methodology of measuring disablism is also addressed by the authors.

A new report says disabled people encounter barriers in access to employment, housing and social care, transport, leisure and status

'Measuring the extent of institutional and cultural prejudice against disabled people is the first step to making disablism history,' says Sarah Gillinson of Demos, one of the report's authors. 'Empowering individual disabled people to use measures of discrimination to highlight and begin tackling the daily injustices they face, is the crucial next step.'

Disablist Britain follows two earlier Scope and DDA commissioned Demos reports: *Disablism: How to tackle the last prejudice* and *Independent Living* as part of Scope's Time to Get Equal campaign. It takes inspiration from Professor Colin Barnes' ground-breaking 1991 work, *Disabled People in Britain and Discrimination*.

Notes

1. *Disablist Britain: Barriers to independent living for disabled people in 2006* by Sarah Gillinson, Julia Huber and Paul Miller is published by Scope with Demos and Disability Awareness in Action on Thursday 9th March 2006. Copies can be downloaded from www.demos.co.uk/publications/disablistbritain

2. Sarah Gillinson and Julia Huber are researchers at Demos. Paul Miller is a Demos Associate.

3. Scope is a national disability organisation whose focus is cerebral palsy. Its aim is that disabled people achieve equality: a society in which they are as valued and have the same human and civil rights as everyone else. www.scope.org.uk

4. *Disablist Britain* is part of Scope's ongoing Time to Get Equal campaign which aims to raise awareness of the problems and barriers faced by disabled people in their everyday lives, demand improvements in the attitudes and actions that disabled people experience and build a mass movement of disabled and non-disabled people campaigning and working towards equality. www.timetogetequal.org.uk

5. Demos is the think-tank for everyday democracy. It has a strong interest in equality and the importance of influencing public attitudes.

6. Disability Awareness in Action (DAA) is an international human rights network, run for and by disabled people. Its aim is to give disabled people information and support material to help them take effective action for themselves.

9 March 2006

⇨ The above information is reprinted with kind permission from Demos. Visit www.demos.co.uk for more information.

© *Demos*

Recognising disablism

Information from TheSite.org

David Bourroughs is a 23-year-old guy who likes pubbing, clubbing, and the rest; and happens to use a wheelchair. Currently volunteering in the Charity Partnerships Fundraising team at disability organisation Scope, David is clocking up experience in order to take the fundraising world by storm!

David believes that racism, in any form, shouldn't be tolerated. But why is it that disablism is still not taken seriously?

It's been hard to ignore the row about Britain's 'intolerance' of bigotry and bullying that engulfed Channel 4's *Celebrity Big Brother* house at the start of 2007. But whatever happened, I hope we all recognise that racism, in whatever form, is wrong and shouldn't be tolerated. I'd like to think that people are just as intolerant about bullying someone because of their age, gender, sexuality or disability. Unfortunately, from personal experience I think that disablism survives as an acceptable and all too common face of bigotry.

If someone used inappropriate language or gestures about someone's disability in the *Big Brother* house, would it have been viewed the same way or provoked the same reaction from the press as the issue of racism did? Or have we in fact already seen disablism rear its head more covertly in the house? Remember the rather patronising way Pete Bennett, the *Big Brother 7* contestant, was treated? Everyone loved Pete. Good old Pete with his 'acceptable' impairment, Tourette's syndrome. They all either wanted to bed him or be his best pal. Most of this was because he was seen as 'vulnerable' or 'sweet' because of his disability (far from the case, he was, erm, very experienced as it turns out), but of course it helped that he was a good-looking lad. Interestingly, Pete seemed to use a mechanism for coping with all this attention – self-deprecation and exaggeration, almost to the point of deliberately 'entertaining' his housemates with his disability. It's like disabled people have to laugh along with the joke, to make everyone else feel comfortable!

'I certainly don't want special treatment – just equal treatment'

Is it wrong to compare racism to disablism? I don't think so. OK, so we haven't seen the levels of victimisation that we witnessed in *Big Brother* against a disabled housemate, but then we still haven't yet had a disabled person with more complicated support needs – or even a wheelchair user – in the house. This is despite many disabled people applying for the show each year.

When I see disabled people in the media it's usually to make a social comment (like in BBC's *Extras*) or to be a tokenistic character. But what's wrong with showing disabled people as incidental characters or even bad people? The BBC3 comedy *I'm With Stupid* is one show to have a go at this. It includes a handful of disabled actors led by Paul Henshall's deliberately unlikeable protagonist. Shocking eh? Disabled people are just like you.

Like racism, I believe it's largely cultural ignorance and a lack of education that leads to discrimination towards disabled people. What gets me is that it's now 2007, and we're still facing staggering ignorance towards people who are seen to be 'different'.

I went to a mainstream school and I think, where possible, this should be the norm for all disabled people – including those with greater support needs. We all have to get along in the wider world, so why educate us separately? How are we supposed to get educated about disability and difference if we don't get a chance to learn side by side, form friendships and hang out? Getting society to accept disabled people at school, at work, and out and about, can only improve things. I certainly don't want special treatment – just equal treatment. Maybe then I wouldn't get people 'tutting' or moaning when the ramp on the bus is taking too long to lower for my wheelchair. That's if the thing works at all. Sorry if I'm inconveniencing your journey!

So *Celebrity Big Brother* has 'done' racism, but will we see a physically disabled housemate enter the Big Brother house in the future? Previously I would have said 'No', but given the recent controversy and publicity that Channel 4 and Endemol have stirred up, I wouldn't be that surprised if a disabled person slipped through soon just so the cynical producers could see what the non-disabled housemates would subject them to! Tasks would have to be accessible, that's for sure. That would stir up the house – but do you know what? If it served to highlight prejudice towards disabled people in the same way as Shilpa Shetty's treatment did for underlying UK racism, then it could be a good thing. Then we would take the first steps to giving disabled people an unmediated voice on TV, and exposing people's prejudices for what they are.

⇨ The above information is reprinted with kind permission from TheSite.org. Visit www.thesite.org for more information.

© *TheSite.org*

Living with a label

Despite long-standing legislation against disability discrimination, serious prejudice and misunderstanding still exist. With one in five adults classed as disabled, a government rethink is needed. Mary O'Hara reports

The Disability Discrimination Act (DDA), which made it on to the statute book in 1995, was a key victory for campaigners. It began a process of securing legal protection from discrimination and raised hopes of transforming society's attitudes toward disabled people. So why does a national survey published 11 years later conclude that the public is confused about what constitutes a disability and that serious prejudice persists?

52% of those surveyed did not think of someone with schizophrenia as being disabled and only 44% regarded an older person with a hearing aid as having a disability

---

The latest *British Social Attitudes Survey*, published today, concludes that disability is still largely perceived in the narrow and outdated sense of visible physical disability, such as wheelchair use, even though the DDA has a much broader definition that incorporates conditions such as long-term debilitating illness. It also reveals worrying levels of prejudice against some groups defined as disabled under the act – in particular, people with mental illness.

According to the study, 52% of those surveyed did not think of someone with schizophrenia as being disabled and only 44% regarded an older person with a hearing aid as having a disability, yet 31% regarded a person with a broken leg who needed to use crutches as disabled.

'The general public tends not to draw the definition as wide as the DDA does,' the report's authors conclude. 'Mental health conditions are often not seen as disabilities. Nor are long-standing illnesses, such as cancer or HIV/AIDS, included by most people.'

But if the public appears confused about what a disability is – under the DDA definition, one in five adults, around 10m, in the UK is disabled – some of the study's findings on perception of prejudice will concern campaigners. According to the survey, 75% of people believe disabled people experience 'a little' prejudice, but only 25% think they face 'a lot'. For many charities and campaign groups, this is far from the reality of everyday life for disabled people.

Face ignorance

In addition, the survey concludes that some groups appear to face ignorance and even fear of their disability. More than 70% of people interviewed said they would 'not feel comfortable' living next door to someone with schizophrenia, and half would not want someone with depression as a neighbour.

There is much confusion when it comes to who is most likely to encounter prejudice. Those groups least likely to be seen by the wider public as disabled are, in fact, perceived as the most discriminated against. For example, 46% of the population believe people with schizophrenia experience a lot of prejudice, yet other groups, such as deaf people, are viewed as facing very little. Some 42% of people believe deaf people experience 'hardly any or no' prejudice and that only 13% face a lot. A spokesman for the RNID says that, for deaf people, the figures are worrying and 'in no way reflect the true extent' of the difficulties faced.

The muddled perceptions exposed by the report, about both the nature of disability and the reality of prejudice, highlight that there is still some way to go to change attitudes to disability.

'Most people say they would not be very comfortable living next door to someone with a mental health condition and the prejudice is more pronounced when they were asked how they would feel if a close relative married someone with a long-term health condition like MS or severe arthritis,' says Bert Massie, chairman of the Disability Rights Commission (DRC). 'These findings catalogue a degree of social repulsion to disabled people that is unparalleled with any other group. If these attitudes are allowed to fester unchecked, we will only be encouraging a segregated society.

'Despite 12 years of disability discrimination legislation, the report reveals that disabled people are still struggling to rid themselves of the tag "second class citizens". We clearly have a long way to go before disabled and non-disabled people work together, learn together, and share the same communities. As countless other examples show, it is only in this way that prejudice is broken down.'

The study's authors argue that their findings could have profound implications for how greater awareness of disability and changes in attitudes are to be achieved in the long term.

The DDA – which has been introduced in stages since 1995 and covers a range of protection against discrimination, including that experienced in employment and education – is regarded by many as a huge step forward in the campaign for disabled rights. So too was the setting up seven years ago of the DRC, with a remit to eradicate discrimination and pursue equal opportunities. They are examples of how the effort behind campaigning has been focused, understandably, on cementing legal rights.

But what needs to be done now? And will the findings in today's report really help shape what happens?

The consensus from charities and campaigners is that the research has highlighted how essential it is not to become complacent. In many ways, it backs up surveys conducted in recent years by the DRC and advocacy groups such as Leonard Cheshire, which found that disabled people continue to experience substantial prejudice in their everyday lives, not just in areas that are legislated for such as the workplace.

A spokesman for Leonard Cheshire says the study may be an indication that while the DDA has helped raise awareness of discrimination, people nevertheless 'still don't seem to fully understand what a disability is'. It is a long-term issue, he says, and one that will require ongoing effort by campaigners. 'You don't just change attitudes the moment a new act is passed.'

Brian Lamb, director of communications at the RNID, agrees. 'I think there needs to be a huge long-term awareness campaign,' he says. 'We're not really going to get change without changes in work, but people need to meet disabled people in social life and other areas.'

Policy initiatives

Many campaigners are also demanding that the government learns a lesson from the survey and puts more resources and cash into campaigns designed to change attitudes, such as anti-stigma campaigns on behalf of people with mental illness. A spokesman for the mental health charity, Mind, says charities cannot do it on their own and that the government should take heed of policy initiatives elsewhere. 'In New Zealand, they have been successful at raising awareness, thanks to high-profile TV campaigns,' he says. 'But it takes money. The sector is very keen to do it, but you can't do it for nothing.'

More than 70% of people interviewed said they would 'not feel comfortable' living next door to someone with schizophrenia, and half would not want someone with depression as a neighbour

---

Despite the pessimistic picture painted by the report, it does include several positive points. For example, it finds that where someone knows or is related to a disabled person, they have a greater understanding of the issues and are much less likely to hold negative attitudes.

The report concludes that this is a clear argument in favour of policy continuing to focus on the inclusion of disabled people in wider society.

Lamb agrees. 'It's getting better. We now have whole generations of children growing up with disabled children in their classroom. This is a very positive thing.'

In February, the DRC will launch its new Disability Agenda, in which it will lay out guidance on the direction that future public policy should take. It has been put together in advance of the body being absorbed in the autumn by the new Commission for Equality and Human Rights and will recommend policies promoting further integration of disabled people into mainstream society. It will aim to 'tackle the most deep-rooted and persistent disadvantage experienced by disabled people', a spokesman says.

But even if the agenda does succeed in injecting a fresh focus into disability policy, campaigners say that government needs to play its part, and that a key lesson to be taken from today's survey is that legislation is merely the beginning.

⇨ The *British Social Attitudes Survey 2006/07* edition is published today by Sage Publications on behalf of the National Centre for Social Research. www.natcen.ac.uk
24 January 2007

Disabled people on TV

Disabled people still under-represented on television – survey

The majority of television viewers say they would like to see more disabled people on screen.

Seventy-seven per cent of those polled said they would not find it offensive to see a disabled person hosting a mainstream TV programme

That's according to a new survey conducted for the Employers' Forum on Disability's Broadcasting & Creative Industries' Disability Network (BCIDN).

The results of a YouGov poll carried out in early October were

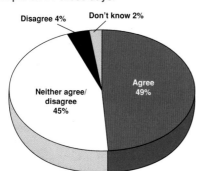

employers'
forum on
disability

announced to senior players in the industry last month.

77 per cent of those polled said they would not find it offensive to see a disabled person hosting a mainstream TV programme and only nine per cent said they wouldn't want to see people with facial disfigurements and 'severe' disabilities in programmes such as soaps or quiz shows.

Other results from the survey included:

⇨ Only four per cent of adults disagreed with the statement that

it is good to see more disabled people on TV these days.

⇨ 78 per cent agreed that they would not be bothered if a disabled person presented the main evening news.

⇨ Only nine per cent disagreed with the statement that there should be more portrayals of disabled people on TV in a wider variety of roles.

The YouGov survey results were based on an online representative sample of 2,716 adults. Fieldwork was conducted from 3rd to 6th October 2006.

7 November 2006

⇨ The above information is reprinted with kind permission from the Employers' Forum on Disability. Visit www.employers-forum.co.uk for more information.

© *Employers' Forum on Disability*

Disabled people on TV: results of the YouGov survey

The YouGov questionnaire asked the question: 'Do you agree with the following statement?' These results followed:

I think it's good that you see more disabled people on TV these days.

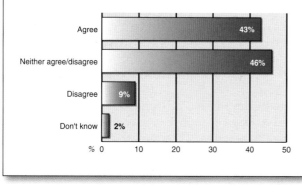

It would not bother me if a disabled person read the main evening news.

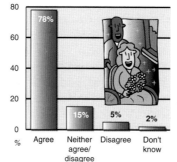

I would find it offensive to see a disabled person hosting a programme like a chat show.

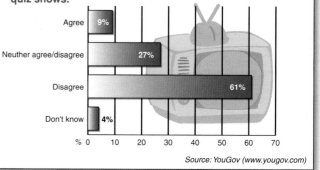

I think there should be more portrayals of disabled people on TV in a wider variety of roles.

I don't want to see people with disfigurements or 'severe' disabilities in mainstream programming such as soaps or quiz shows.

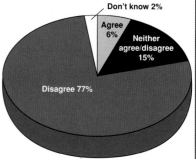

Source: YouGov (www.yougov.com)

Information on learning disabilities

Information from Mencap

What is a learning disability?

A learning disability affects the way someone learns, communicates or does some everyday things. Someone has a learning disability all through their life.

There are many different types of learning disability. They can be mild, moderate or severe.

Some people with a mild learning disability do not need a lot of support in their lives. But other people may need support with all sorts of things, like getting dressed, going shopping, or filling out forms.

Some people with a learning disability also have a physical disability. This can mean they need a lot of support 24 hours a day.

A learning disability does not stop someone from learning and achieving a lot in life, if they get the right support.

What causes learning disability?

There are many different causes of learning disability. Often it is not possible to say why someone has a learning disability. But most learning disabilities are caused by the way the brain develops – before, during or soon after birth:

Before birth
⇨ things that happen to the central nervous system (the brain and the spinal cord).
⇨ the mother having an accident or illness when she is pregnant.
⇨ the genes that a parent passes on or how the genes develop while the unborn baby develops (genes are chemicals in our bodies that contain information about us – like how we look).

During birth
⇨ when a baby does not get enough oxygen or is born too early.

After birth
⇨ early childhood illnesses or physical accidents.

Common causes of learning disability

Here is some information about the most common causes of inherited learning disability. (Inherited means that it is passed down from parents to children in their 'genes'.)

These are not different types of learning disability. But people who have these conditions are likely to have a learning disability.

Fragile X syndrome
⇨ Fragile X syndrome is the most common cause of inherited learning disability.
⇨ Not all people with Fragile X syndrome have a learning disability. If they do, the learning disability could be mild, moderate or severe.
⇨ It is usually possible to tell if someone has Fragile X syndrome from their facial appearance (the way they look).
⇨ People with Fragile X syndrome may also have problems with:
– concentration communicating and relating to other people.

Down's syndrome
⇨ Down's syndrome is a genetic condition. It is caused by an extra chromosome in a person's cells. (All living things are made up of 'cells'. Chromosomes are parts of cells.)
⇨ All people who have Down's syndrome have some kind of learning disability.
⇨ It is usually possible to tell if someone has Down's syndrome from their facial appearance (the way they look).
⇨ Down's syndrome is not an illness or a disease.
⇨ About 60,000 people in the UK have Down's syndrome.
⇨ 1 out of every 1,000 babies born has Down's syndrome.

Important facts about learning disability

A learning disability can affect someone's life a lot. This is partly because people with a learning disability may find it harder to understand things than other people.

But it is also because other people often do not understand what it means for someone to have a learning disability. As a result people with a learning disability often do not get treated properly.

Here are some important facts about learning disability:
⇨ 1.5 million people in the UK have a learning disability.
⇨ 200 babies are born with a learning disability every week.
⇨ Nine out of 10 people with a learning disability get bullied.
⇨ There are more than 29,000 people with a severe or profound learning disability who live at home with carers aged over 70.

Some conditions often associated with learning disability

Cerebral palsy

⇨ Cerebral palsy is a physical condition (to do with the body). It affects people's movement. It can be mild, moderate or severe.

⇨ Cerebral palsy is not a learning disability, but many people with a learning disability also have cerebral palsy.

Epilepsy

⇨ Epilepsy is a neurological condition (to do with the body's nervous system). It is not a learning disability, but about 30% of people with a learning disability also have epilepsy.

⇨ People with epilepsy have fits. A fit happens when there is a problem with activity in the brain.

Autism

⇨ Autism is a lifelong disability that affects the way someone communicates and relates to people around them.

⇨ Autism is not a learning disability, but people with autism often have a learning disability. They face similar problems and have similar needs to people with a learning disability.

⇨ Someone's autism can be mild, moderate, or severe.

⇨ It is not possible to tell from the way someone looks if they have autism.

⇨ People with autism may have difficulties with:
   ↳ forming relationships with other people
   ↳ communicating and understanding what other people are trying to communicate
   ↳ using their imagination.

⇨ About 91 in every 10,000 people in the UK have autism.

Asperger's syndrome

⇨ Asperger's syndrome is a form of autism. Like autism, it is not a learning disability, but it can affect the way someone communicates and relates to other people.

⇨ People with Asperger's syndrome can find it dificult to tell how other people are feeling by looking at the expression on their faces or listening to the tone of their voices.

⇨ People with Asperger's syndrome usually have fewer problems with language than people with autism.

⇨ People with Asperger's syndrome are less likely to have a learning disability than people with autism. So they often have average or above-average intelligence.

⇨ People with Asperger's syndrome often like to have a regular routine every day and can find changes to this upsetting.

Accessed 22 March 2007

⇨ The above information is reprinted with kind permission from Mencap. Visit www.mencap.org.uk for more information.

© Mencap

Managing a learning disability

It may last a lifetime, but living with a learning disability doesn't have to hold you back

In every case, a person with a learning disability needs help to identify their areas of weakness, and then use their strengths to compensate. This is where outside support and assistance comes in, and not just in the form of professionals. Everyone from family to friends, teachers, tutors, work colleagues and employers can help. How? By being aware of the person's learning disability, and any coping strategies that can help them reach their true potential.

If you're living with a learning disability and still in education, it's vital that you make your school or college aware of your situation. By talking openly about your needs, they can look into ways to tackle any difficulties you're having.

Many people with learning disabilities benefit from supplementary

education. This can be tailored to suit your individual needs, but ranges from extra tuition to simply creating a home environment where problems at school or college can be discussed. Even being encouraged to read or write outside of the classroom or lecture hall can be a big benefit.

By becoming aware of your strengths and weaknesses, it's possible to fulfil your potential in all areas of life. The same goes for anyone

caring for somebody with a learning disability. What matters is that you constantly review the situation, and remain aware of any source of help, encouragement and support that's available.

Supporting yourself

If you're living at home with a learning disability and you're keen to make the most of your independence, it's vital you learn the basic skills to take care of yourself. This begins by talking to your parent(s) or carer, and considering the following areas:

⇨ Living alone – If you're thinking about moving out, is suitable accommodation available? Will anyone be looking out for you? Do you need help with specific tasks, such as dealing with a central heating system?

- Domestic duties – Are you able to keep the place clean and secure?
- Preparing meals – Can you cook for yourself? Are you aware of basic standards of hygiene and safety? Do you need help with grocery shopping?
- Money matters – Are you financially independent? Can you live on a budget and pay bills on time?

- Getting around – Are you confident using public transport? Are you able to get yourself from A to B without problems? Alternatively, are you equipped with strategies for dealing with difficulties i.e. carrying a mobile phone with the number of someone who can help you out?

The prospect may seem daunting for some, but over time and with support it's possible for anyone with a learning disability to achieve a degree of independence and freedom that suits them.

- The above information is reprinted with kind permission from TheSite.org. Visit www.thesite.org for more information.

© TheSite.org

Not seen, not heard

People with a learning disability are still 'Not seen, not heard' in the media

The BBC launched *Not seen, not heard* today, 25.1.06. The report shows that people with a learning disability are major consumers of the media and want to get their news, information and entertainment presented in an accessible way on television, radio and the internet.

There are around 1.5 million people with a learning disability in the UK

Jo Williams, chief executive of Mencap, said:

'We look forward to seeing how the BBC and other broadcasters respond to the findings in the report. We hope they will include more information about issues relevant to people with a learning disability and present these in a way that is accessible to people with a learning disability, incorporating their views in programming.

'We know that people with a learning disability are currently under-represented in the media. We hope broadcasters will take the opportunity to show the talent and unique experiences of people with a learning disability. We'd like to see them inviting actors with a learning disability to take roles in soaps and participate in TV shows. We encourage broadcasters to

MENCAP
Understanding learning disability

give employment to people with a learning disability both on and off screen. It will be a fantastic result if this report makes a difference.'

Ciara Evans, Mencap's celebrity research assistant who has a learning disability and who took part in the BBC research, commented:

'It's great the research has happened. Hopefully, from now on, the media will be more positive about including people with a learning disability.'

The launch took place at BBC Television Centre in London and was attended by guests who took part in the research. The launch included a disco hosted by Mencap ambassador and Radio 1 DJ Jo Whiley, together with her sister Frances Whiley, who has a learning disability.

Notes
- Mencap works with people with a learning disability and their families and carers, fighting to end discrimination and prejudice, and providing a wide range of quality services.
- There are around 1.5 million people with a learning disability in the UK.
- Learning disabilities have many different causes but are always lifelong. A learning disability can affect someone's life in many ways, causing difficulties in learning, communicating or doing everyday things. A learning disability does not prevent someone from learning and achieving a lot in life, if given the right support.
- For information about learning disability issues please call the Learning Disability Helpline (England) on 0808 808 1111 or visit www.askmencap.info

25 January 2006

- The above information is reprinted with kind permission from Mencap. Visit www.mencap.org.uk for more information.

© Mencap

Special Educational Needs

Information from Contact a Family

What are Special Educational Needs?

Special Educational Needs (SEN) has a legal definition. Children with SEN have learning difficulties or disabilities that make it harder for them to learn than most children of the same age. These children may need extra or different help from that given to other children of the same age. The SEN Code of Practice for England legally defines children with SEN as children who have a considerably greater difficulty in learning than others the same age. It also includes children who cannot use the educational facilities which other children of a similar age use because of their disability. Children under school age who would fall into either category without extra help are also included.

Types of school/ education provision

⇨ Academies: An independent state school which is set up to replace a failing school or where a new school is needed and which specialises in particular curriculum areas. Academies can be named on a Statement but cannot be forced to admit a child by the SEN and Disability Tribunal because of their independent status.

⇨ City Colleges: A school which operates as an independent state school and is jointly funded by the government and private sponsorship. They may operate their own admission criteria which all pupils, including those with SEN, must satisfy.

> **Children with SEN have learning difficulties or disabilities that make it harder for them to learn than most children of the same age**

⇨ Foundation schools: A school which receives funding via the local authority but retains control of their own administration. When grant maintained schools were abolished most became foundation schools.

⇨ Independent schools: A school which is not maintained by an LEA and charges fees but may be approved by the Secretary of State as being suitable for children with special educational needs. Independent schools are not covered by much of the law governing schools, but the Disability Discrimination Act does apply.

⇨ Maintained schools: A school maintained by an LEA, including community, voluntary aided and foundation schools.

⇨ Non-maintained special schools: A special school in England which is not maintained by an LEA and charges fees. They are usually run by a charity or charitable trust.

⇨ Portage: Home based educational support for pre-school children with special educational needs.

⇨ Pupil Referral Unit (PRU): A school or other educational provision maintained by an LEA to provide education for pupils who are not able to attend mainstream school because of illness, exclusion or other reason.

⇨ Special school: A school exclusively for children with special educational needs.

⇨ The above information is reprinted with kind permission from Contact a Family. Information applies to England. Please visit their website www.cafamily.org for more information.

© Contact a Family

Learning together for the better

Despite evidence that mainstream education works for disabled pupils, the debate on whether inclusion could work for all persists. Priya Kotecha investigates the barriers and how they could be brought down

Preethi Manuel fought hard to secure mainstream schooling for her daughter Zahrah, who has high support needs and is now 19.

She believed so strongly in mainstream education that she taught Zahrah at home, while fighting a tribunal against her local education authority (LEA), which insisted Zahrah should attend a special school.

'Inclusion is where everyone feels that they are part of a society where they can contribute and give back to society'

Mrs Manuel visited the school chosen by the LEA, but found it unsuitable. She says: 'There wasn't an awful lot of aural or visual stimulation for her, which is very important as Zahrah is non-verbal.

'I knew that once she had gone in, it would have been very difficult to get her out.'

The tribunal asked Camden LEA to reconsider its position, but it would not. Only a sit-in protest by parents of disabled children prompted the LEA to offer a programme where Zahrah attended her local mainstream primary school for two days and was educated at home for the other three.

Within a term, Zahrah was attending full-time, thanks to the help of teaching assistants who adapted the curriculum for Zahrah's abilities and Mrs Manuel's perseverance.

'As each child is different so are their needs'

She says: 'As soon as she went in, the barriers came down. The teachers were excellent and the pupils were very warm with her.'

Mrs Manuel believes all disabled children, regardless of their impairment, could be educated in mainstream settings.

She adds: 'If it can be done for my daughter, whom professionals had written off, then inclusion is possible for anyone.'

But Baroness Warnock – once thought to be a champion of inclusive education – questions moves to include children with severe behavioural, emotional and social difficulties (BESD), including those with autism and Asperger's syndrome.

At a Scope conference in June, she said: 'I believe that it is little short of cruelty to insist on ideological grounds that those children should be subjected to the torment of a mainstream school even if it is for the sake of the good of other children who will learn that such strange people exist.'

Mrs Manuel believes Baroness Warnock is confused about what inclusion means.

She says: 'Inclusion is where everyone feels that they are part of a society where they can contribute and give back to society – that's what inclusion is about.'

Organisations representing people with BESD and learning difficulties question whether mainstream schools can provide inclusive education for all – even with improved resources.

Jo Williams, chief executive of Mencap, says inclusion for children with learning difficulties can work, but points out that mainstream schools need to improve their education standards for such pupils.

She adds: 'As each child is different so are their needs – some will thrive in an atmosphere of inclusion while others will do better in special schools.'

The National Autistic Society (NAS) believes parents should not have to choose between mainstream and special school provision, but concentrate on putting children's interests first.

Amanda Batten, NAS policy and campaigns officer for children, says: 'The key issues that everyone will agree on are more training for teachers, more support for children and better-resourced provision. Children are often coming to our schools after they've fallen out of mainstream schools, which shows that mainstream provision is not suitable for everyone.'

The Commons education select committee is just one group that has recently published a report demanding improvements in special educational needs (SEN) provision. It highlights the 'postcode lottery' of provision and calls for a 'clear over-arching strategy for SEN and disability policy'.

But the committee does not call for a fully inclusive education, rather a 'broad range of high quality, well-resourced, flexible provision to meet the needs of all children'.

Research published at the same time as the select committee report – by Ofsted – found that children with SEN have a better chance of developing their academic, personal and social skills in well-resourced mainstream schools than other educational settings.

It says while many disabled children learn well both in mainstream and special schools, there was 'more good and outstanding provision in resourced mainstream schools'.

Researchers found fewer pupils with severe or multiple learning difficulties were placed in mainstream schools than other groups, even where specialist provision was available. With these pupils and those with challenging behaviour, it says: 'Given specialist resources and teaching in a well-resourced mainstream school, they were able to make outstanding progress.'

Tara Flood, director at the Alliance for Inclusive Education, says the research should be used to push forward the inclusive education agenda that calls for all disabled children to be given access to mainstream schools.

'We must use this evidence to convince the government that it must focus on capacity building mainstream schools so they can better include a more diverse range of learners.'

She says those who support special schools have a 'vested interest' in maintaining the status quo and does not believe parents would choose them unless told by a professional that their child's needs would be best met there.

Mark Vaughan, founder and co-director of the Centre for Studies on Inclusive Education, says: 'The anti-inclusion lobby should justify its stance on segregation rather than the inclusion movement justifying it on inclusion.'

He says the expert knowledge developed in special schools had been instrumental in helping mainstream schools to be more inclusive, but adds the 'government should now clearly indicate that inclusion is a wider policy than just including disabled kids [where they can fit now]'.

Other changes [within schools] should include celebrating difference within society and for everyone to work towards a philosophy that focuses on the individual child

---

Where the right investment and planning has occurred disabled children can thrive in mainstream settings – according to Brigid Jackson Dooley, headmistress of Cleves Primary School in Newham.

The London borough is hailed as a shining example of where inclusion is working well to the benefit of all children.

Ms Jackson Dooley says for inclusion to work, schools must change their managerial, organisational and structural procedures to fit around children with SEN.

She says: 'We have to change the school and not the child. There are several things that need to change for inclusion to happen. We need a greater understanding of measures of success. There is this perception that success can only be based on attainment, but it should be based on progression, for example, how far a disabled child's communication skills have developed.'

She says other changes should include celebrating difference within society and for everyone to work towards a philosophy that focuses on the individual child.

Richard Reiser, director of Disability Equality in Education, says: 'We now have sufficient examples and experience to demonstrate that inclusion can work for all pupils regardless of the type or degree of their impairment. Educationalists need to learn from this experience.'

Learning materials are spreading – as with the guide *Implementing The DDA in Schools and Early Years Settings*, from the Department for Education and Skills – but Mr Reiser hopes to see significant improvements through the Disability Discrimination Act's new equality duties (DED) – requiring public bodies to tackle inequality – which will be enforced in December. This year, LEAs and mainstream secondary schools must have their equality schemes in place; all other institutions must do so by December 2007.

He says: 'The DED will start on a low impact. For a start, most schools don't know about it. But it will build

up its impact as a few schools and LEAs get judicially reviewed for failure to have adequate schemes.'

He stresses – contrary to some campaigners – that co-location of special schools or units on mainstream campuses for children cannot be called inclusion, merely 'forms of social integration'.

Mr Reiser says: 'The main way in which children build relationships with peers and support each other in their learning is [in] the class or teaching group and this needs to be organised in such a way that all children regardless of their impairment can take part in learning and social activities.'

'Every disabled child has a right to receive the individual care, support and education they need, within a non-segregated setting'

Scope says it is attempting to bridge the gap between those who push for total inclusion and those who question how it can work, by exploring and developing practical models. Through its arm Scope Inc, it uses expertise developed in specialist education to integrate disabled children into mainstream settings such as their local school.

To make such models work, the charity says the government must remove provisions in the Education Act which allow mainstream education to be refused if a placement will affect 'the provision of efficient education for other children' – as these make it too easy for schools to deny disabled children their right to inclusion.

Andy Lusk, Scope's director of education and early years, says: 'Every disabled child has a right to receive the individual care, support and education they need, within a non-segregated setting.

'Scope is looking beyond the mainstream versus special schools debate to find solutions which really work for children with the most complex additional needs.'

Rosemarie Mason, from Ilford, passionately supports inclusive education, but did not attempt to get it for her son Sean, now 18, who has more severe autism than her other children, Eoin and Micheal.

She says: 'We knew it wouldn't happen anyway. We got him a very good school that was autism specific, so he got integration that way, but it's not ideal.'

Now, she adds: 'It's more acceptable for [disabled] kids to go to mainstream schools, but even after the first review, they are guiding you to a special school. Mainstream schools don't want kids like mine,' she adds.

Keeping Eoin in a mainstream school has also been difficult, particularly because he was bullied.

'In general educational establishments don't look at individuals. I think you can work with a whole group of kids but individualise it too. It's down to the attitude.'

Carole Burgess says inclusion has worked well for her 12-year-old disabled daughter Rachel, because the school she attends takes an individualised approach towards including disabled children.

Rachel – who has global developmental delay – and her non-disabled brother Edward attend Cleves Primary School in Newham.

She says: 'The school fits around Rachel, rather than her fitting into the school.

'Whatever they do in the classroom, they involve her as much as possible. They also have a sensory room and large play area – as a result her communication has developed well. She's limited by what she can do physically, but they make every effort to involve her in drama, music and PE.

'Cleves was built originally to be inclusive. That makes a lot of difference, because if you have Victorian buildings, so much money has to be spent on making the buildings accessible.'
September 2006

⇨ Information from *Disability Now* (www.disabilitynow.org.uk). To subscribe to *Disability Now* and for a free sample copy, contact: 0845 130 9177, email: dnsubs@ servicehelpline.co.uk

© *Disability Now*

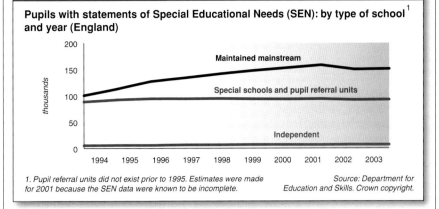

Special Educational Needs

Pupils with statements of Special Educational Needs (SEN): by type of school[1] and year (England)

- Maintained mainstream
- Special schools and pupil referral units
- Independent

1. Pupil referral units did not exist prior to 1995. Estimates were made for 2001 because the SEN data were known to be incomplete.

Source: Department for Education and Skills. Crown copyright.

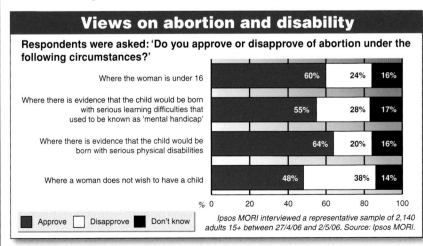

Views on abortion and disability

Respondents were asked: 'Do you approve or disapprove of abortion under the following circumstances?'

	Approve	Disapprove	Don't know
Where the woman is under 16	60%	24%	16%
Where there is evidence that the child would be born with serious learning difficulties that used to be known as 'mental handicap'	55%	28%	17%
Where there is evidence that the child would be born with serious physical disabilities	64%	20%	16%
Where a woman does not wish to have a child	48%	38%	14%

Ipsos MORI interviewed a representative sample of 2,140 adults 15+ between 27/4/06 and 2/5/06. Source: Ipsos MORI.

INDEX

academies, Special Educational Needs provision 36
access
  problems 3
  requirements, Disability Discrimination Act 22
adjusting to disability 4
air travel 9
Asperger's syndrome 34
assisted dying bill 24
attitudes to disability 1, 30-31
autism 34

benefits 3, 4, 5-6
blue badge scheme 7-8
books, portraying disabled children 21
bus travel 8-9

care component, Disability Living Allowance 5
care gap 20
carers, young 10-12
cerebral palsy and learning disabilities 34
concessionary fares 8, 9
costs of disability 5, 17, 18

developing countries
  and disability rights 26-7
  disability statistics 25
dial-a bus schemes 8
disability
  costs of 17, 18
  definition 2
  and the media 29, 32, 35
  and poverty 16, 17-18
  worldwide statistics 25
  UK statistics 1, 2-3, 6
Disability Agenda, DRC 16, 31
disability discrimination see discrimination
Disability Discrimination Act (DDA) 13, 22, 31
  and schools 38-9
Disability Employment Advisers 4
Disability Equality Duty (DED) 13
  and schools 38-9
Disability Living Allowance (DLA) 5
disability rights, UN treaty 26
Disability Rights Commission 16, 31
  Independence Day report 20
Disability Rights Handbook 6
disability symbol 14
disabled children
  choice in education 24-5
  in developing countries 26
  resources for 21
  violence against 27
disabled person's railcard 8
Disabled Person's Tax Credit 5
disablism 28-9
  see also discrimination

discrimination 1, 3
  Disability Discrimination Act 13, 22, 31, 38-9
  workplace 15
diversity as business benefit 14
doctors 4
Down's syndrome and learning disabilities 33
DRC see Disability Rights Commission
driving 4, 7

education
  children with learning disabilities 36-9
  choice for disabled children 24-5
  developing countries 26
employment 15
  disability symbol 14
  rates 3
  rights 4
epilepsy and learning disabilities 34
equality rights for disabled people 13
escort services 9

family, effect of disability on 4
financial support see benefits
foundation schools 36
Fragile X syndrome 33

gender and disability 2
government support for disability awareness 31
GPs and disability support 4

health care services 4
help see support
Hidden Lives report 11
Housing Benefit 5

Improving the Life Chances of Disabled People 23-4
Incapacity Benefit (ICB) 5
inclusive education 37-9
Income Support (IS) 5
Independence Day report 20
independent living and learning disabilities 34-5
independent schools and SEN provision 36
Industrial Injuries Disablement Benefit 5
information for disabled children 21
inherited learning disability 33
institutional disablism 28
Invalid Care Allowance (ICA) 5-6

language describing disabled people 1
learning disabilities 33-9
  causes 33
  definition 33
  management of 34-5
  and the media 35
  statistics 33
Leonard Cheshire Disabled People's Forum 15

mainstream education and disabled children 37-9
maintained schools 36
media
  and learning disabilities 35
  portrayal of disabled people 29, 32
medical model of disability 1
mental health
  effects of disability 4
  issues awareness 23
Microsoft, Workability initiative 15
minicabs 9
mobility component, Disability Living Allowance 5
motoring and disability 7

non-maintained special schools 36
Not seen, not Heard report 35

Office for Disability Issues (ODI) 23-4

parking concessions 7-8
portage educational support 36
portrayal of disabled people
  in children's books 21
  in the media 29, 32, 35
poverty and disabled people 16-18
prejudice 30-31
  in the workplace 15
public transport 8
pupil referral units 36

rail travel 8
Red Cross Escort service 9
regional patterns of disability 2
religious groups and disability 2
reproductive rights, disabled people 27
resources for disabled children 21
road tax exemption 7

schools see education
Scope, support for inclusive education 39
Severe Disablement Allowance (SDA) 5
sexual rights, disabled people 27
Sharing Information with Disabled Children in the

Early Years 21
Social Attitudes Survey and disability 30
social care services 4
  expectations of 18
  insufficiency 20
Social Fund 5
social model of disability 1
social security benefits see benefits
socio-economic class and disability 2
Special Educational Needs (SEN) 36
  and mainstream schooling 37-9
special schools 36
St John Patient Transport Service, Wales 9
Statutory Sick Pay (SSP) 5
storybooks for disabled children 21
support 4
  financial see benefits
  insufficiency of services 18
  for young carers 10

taxis 9
television and disabled people 29, 32, 35
Thistle Travel card scheme 9
training for disabled people 15
transport 7-9

underground travel 9
unemployment, disabled people 3
United Nations, treaty on disability rights 26

vaccine damage compensation 5
vehicle adaptation 7
violence against disabled people 27

war, effect on disabled people 26
welfare reform bill 23
wheelchairs 7
women, disabled, violence against 27
work see employment
Workability project 15
workplace prejudice 15

young carers 10-12

Additional Resources

Other Issues titles

If you are interested in researching further some of the issues raised in *Coping with Disability*, you may like to read the following titles in the **Issues** series:

⇨ Vol. 128 *The Cannabis Issue* (ISBN 978 1 86168 374 8)
⇨ Vol. 126 *The Abortion Debate* (ISBN 978 1 86168 365 6)
⇨ Vol. 113 *Fitness and Health* (ISBN 978 1 86168 346 5)
⇨ Vol. 110 *Poverty* (ISBN 978 1 86168 343 4)
⇨ Vol. 105 *Ageing Issues* (ISBN 978 1 86168 325 0)

For more information about these titles, visit our website at www.independence.co.uk/publicationslist

Useful organisations

You may find the websites of the following organisations useful for further research:

⇨ Action on Disability and Development: www.add.org.uk
⇨ Arthritis Care: www.arthritiscare.org.uk
⇨ Citizens' Advice: www.adviceguide.org.uk
⇨ Disability Alliance: www.disabilityalliance.org
⇨ Disability Now: www.disabilitynow.org.uk
⇨ Disability Rights Commission: www.drc-gb.org
⇨ Mencap: www.mencap.org.uk
⇨ Scope: www.scope.org.uk
⇨ Shaw Trust: www.shaw-trust.org.uk
⇨ youreable.com: www.youreable.com

ACKNOWLEDGEMENTS

The publisher is grateful for permission to reproduce the following material.

While every care has been taken to trace and acknowledge copyright, the publisher tenders its apology for any accidental infringement or where copyright has proved untraceable. The publisher would be pleased to come to a suitable arrangement in any such case with the rightful owner.

Chapter One: Disability Issues

Disability issues, © Scope, *Disability in the UK*, © ESRC, *Adjusting to disability*, © Crown copyright is reproduced with the permission of Her Majesty's Stationery Office, *Benefits*, © youreable.com, *Disability facts*, © Shaw Trust, *Transport options for disabled people*, © Citizens' Advice, *Young carers*, © TheSite.org, '*Hidden Lives*', © Barnardo's, *Ross's story*, © Princess Royal Trust for Carers.

Chapter Two: Equality and Rights

Equality rights, © Arthritis Care, *The disability symbol*, © Employers' Forum on Disability, *Diversity good for business*, © Disability Now, *Workplace prejudice*, © Leonard Cheshire, *Disabled people continue to bear brunt of UK poverty*, © Disability Rights Commission, *Disability and employment statistics*, © Shaw Trust, *The cost of poverty*, © Paul Treloar/Disability Alliance, *Social care*, © Ipsos MORI, *Expectations of adult social care*, © Ipsos MORI, *The care gap*, © Disability Rights Commission, *Resources for disabled children*, © Scope, *The Disability Discrimination Act*, © Crown copyright is reproduced with the permission of Her Majesty's Stationery Office, *The campaign for real choice*, © Guardian Newspapers Ltd, '*Lack of choice*' *for disabled children*, © Scope, *International disability facts*, © Action on Disability and Development, *Disabled treaty to reverse years of neglect*, © Child Rights Information Network, '*Institutional disablism*' *is rife in Britain*, © Demos, *Recognising disablism*, © TheSite.org, *Living with a label*, © Guardian Newspapers Ltd, *Disabled people on TV*, © Employers' Forum on Disability.

Chapter Three: Learning Disabilities

Information on learning disabilities, © Mencap, *Managing a learning disability*, © TheSite.org, *Not seen, not heard*, © Mencap, *Special Educational Needs*, © Contact a Family, *Learning together for the better*, © Disability Now.

Illustrations

Pages 1, 17, 23, 36: Simon Kneebone; pages 2, 18: Bev Aisbett; pages 10, 20, 27: Angelo Madrid; pages 12, 21, 31, 38: Don Hatcher.

Photographs

Page 5: Carlos Zaragoza; page 9: Ove Töpfer; page 22: Meghan Anderson-Colangelo; page 27: Jyn Meyer; page 33: Vicky Shepherd; page 35: Jenny Hardie; page 37: Paul Gwyther.

And with thanks to the team: Mary Chapman, Sandra Dennis and Jan Haskell.

Lisa Firth
Cambridge
April, 2007